# The IEP PRIMER and the Individualized Program

## Preschool Through Postsecondary Transition



**Beverly A. School, PhD**
**Arlene Cooper, PhD**

Academic Therapy Publications
20 Commercial Boulevard
Novato, California 94949-6191

International Standard Book Number: 0-87879-956-7

2 1 0 9 8 7 6 5 4 3
1 0 9 8 7 6 5 4 3 2

# Contents

# Preface

After ten years, the well-organized *IEP Primer* remains relevant and practical. However, the authors felt a need to address the many recent changes in special education. For one thing, a whole new category, early childhood, has entered the field, and recent federal legislation changes mandate IEPs for developmentally delayed preschool youngsters. Another extension of the Education of the Handicapped Amendment Act of 1990 is a required "transition IEP" to address the vocational and adult life-skill needs of post-secondary students with disabilities.

In general, the IEP concept remains the same, but many of the tools are more sophisticated, such as assessments, program implementation, and new mandates. For that reason, we felt the time had come to update terminology, data, and mandated additions.

Mainstreaming has become a central issue in special education with a whole new "cottage industry" devoted to training regular educators to work with special students. Mainstreaming (sometimes called Integration or Normalization) calls for students with disabilities to spend time with their non-disabled peers in a regular educational setting. When appropriate, Full Inclusion (also called Full Integration), where a disabled student receives his/her total education within the regular classroom setting, is sometimes recommended. The principle intent of Least Restrictive Environment is that each student served by the Individuals with Disabilities Act (IDEA), formerly PL94-142, is placed in the least restrictive environment that meets his or her needs as defined by the IEP.

This update is intended to address practical issues of current IEPs and procedures. Some issues may be brought up, but there is no attempt to offer solutions in this book. Its main purpose is to:

— assist new teachers
— help teachers returning to work after several years of absence
— assist a teacher transferring or newly involved with special education

In other words, this is truly a *primer* for those who will be facing their first IEP. This guide will also be extremely helpful to those who are looking for ideas to develop preschool or transition IEPs in responses to changes in the public law.

In summary, our model was developed to address basic skill needs in a school setting. We are convinced that the expanded and changing needs in special education are a challenge to educators, and our mission is to help meet that ongoing challenge.

We would like to acknowledge the contribution of several colleagues: Michol Berrigan, instructional advisor; Carole De Julio, master teacher; and Sharon Greb, master teacher.

## CHAPTER ONE

# Why IEP?

The intent of this manual is to help teachers formulate and implement individual educational programs (IEP) for each special education student. What was once a program option has now become federal law (formerly PL94-142, now IDEA, Individuals with Disabilities Educational Act, Part B, August 19, 1991, from the Education for All Handicapped Children Act of 1975). Guidelines for the individual programming have been defined by federal legislation.

The idea of an IEP is not new. Many programs for handicapped and nonhandicapped are based on the idea that each child deserves an individual program, but recognizing individual differences or implementing individual programs is far more critical with handicapped students; therefore, the use of individual programs is more prevalent in special education than in regular education. If you believe that every child deserves a program designed for his own level of ability, learning mode, interest, and pace, then you would agree that individual programming is superior to traditional planning. If you believe this is true for every child, it is especially true for special education children.

With the best intentions in the world, teachers have not found it easy to design individual programming. Lacking structure and guidance, many teachers have simply taught reduced or watered down curricula in the same old standard approach and have put great emphasis on making students feel good about themselves. Worthy as this goal is, it has too often been used as an excuse for ineffective teaching. Special education children are identified and placed on the basis of their special needs, and it is incumbent on all teachers to meet these needs with specific instruction instead of well-intended circumventions. Rather than leave good intentions to chance, the Education for All Handicapped Children Act of 1975 (IDEA, formerly known as PL94-142) is mandating that educators provide a program that is both educationally relevant and accountable for each handicapped student. The goals of the law will not be easy to meet.

With federal legislation and funding tied directly to implementation in IDEA (formerly PL94-142), the need to be proficient in individual programming is crucial. Most special education teachers, however, are simply not sufficiently trained in writing IEPs. Even expert teachers who have operated successful individual programs are not trained to project those programs into the IEP format.

Unlike many school districts throughout the United States, we were fortunate in anticipating the mandates of IDEA (formerly PL94-142) quite early as our program for special education developed. Our program had its 20th anniversary in September of 1987. It had begun in 1967 in two rooms, with all children being labeled brain injured. There was a heavy emphasis on perceptual training, under the assumption that academic growth would follow naturally. As the program grew, useful techniques began to emerge. There was little guidance from experts in the beginning, so development came from within the program. Currently, our program covers a county-wide operation in which three thousand students are served throughout several school districts. All classes are located in regular public schools under the label "Learning Disabled" (LD). For the most part, all students are based in regular home rooms and are integrated to the fullest extent possible. The learning disabilities teacher is held responsible for all necessary academic remediation. Aides do some direct perceptual work, but most perceptual work is integrated into the academic program.

The program called for teachers to make an academic assessment. Experience indicated that many teachers were unable to interpret test information or break down the tested skills into discrete educational tasks. For example, some teachers would recognize a tested weakness but not be aware of the various components of the skills tested. At that point, checklists were provided that focused on the smallest unit that could be taught academically. However inadvertently we had begun it, by the time IDEA (formerly PL94-142) became law, we had structured our program to train teachers to assess students individually to determine the specific skill deficits and to formulate a written program for the year. Parents were then contacted for a one-to-one conference, at which time the teacher's findings could be presented and discussed. Parents were also presented with a written program of remediation for the year. This immediately became "an IEP."

The entire concept of IDEA (PL94-142) is predicated on the rights of citizens to a public education/right to treatment; due process—the legal process—has now become part of federal law.

The Education of the Handicapped Amendments Act of 1990 has further extended the mandates, and while the states have interpreted them with different degrees of enthusiasm due to funding problems, there is little dispute that the services for handicapped students has been extended in the public school system. There is now a requirement for a transition IEP to carry handicapped students into adulthood and prepared for the world of adult work and adult living. The transition plans must be completed by the student's sixteenth birthday, and be a blueprint for the educational or vocational needs of the student to meet after-school life. Theoretically, these plans might be extended into full adulthood for ongoing needs. They must cover living arrangements as well as "education" and could vastly extend the role of educators. A full treatment of this law is beyond the scope of this book, but educators need to be aware that IEPs may extend in time indefinitely and be inter-agency based. This will depend, to a large part, on the response of the individual states to the various mandates.

This *Primer* addresses the educator's task of devising an IEP that is relevant for the student in a school setting. We have a decided academic bias from extensive experience, but believe the basic concept can be generalized to non-academic training, based on task analysis and the basic principles of teaching.

## Due Process

Due process is a concept in special education predating IDEA (PL 94-142). Due process evolved from the consent agreement that was filed by the Parents Association of Retarded Children/Citizens (PARC) in 1972. Essentially, due process protects the child's rights to a free public education. As a result of this law, our state implemented a total program to search out and serve all handicapped retarded children. Procedurally, a format was established to integrate the parents in educational planning. The state provided strict guidelines, forms, formats, hearing officers, surrogate parents, and even legal services, all to insure that a child's rights are safeguarded. Due process has provided the vehicle to insure that every child would have service, but that no child would be labeled inappropriately.

## The Notice of Recommended Assignment—(NORA)

NORA is an integral part of the child's due process. The NORA is the document that is presented to parents at the conclusion of an IEP. The signature on the NORA indicates agreement with the individualized program and permission to take the child out of regular education for specified instruction or provide it in the regular classroom. Printed on the face of the NORA are the conditions for parent approval or disapproval. With the initial NORA, a multi-page attachment spells out all the rights of the students and all the procedures involved in due process, including hearing procedures, advisory names and addresses, financial prerogatives, obligations and testing options. NORAs must be legally renewed for two-year intervals, but local practice in many places is to offer a new NORA with each IEP. Should there not be agreement over the IEP, the parent can check (disapprove) rather that approve. In Pennsylvania that automatically triggers a pre-hearing conference. Every effort is made to negotiate positively with parents since districts are reluctant to be adversarial with their own constituents, with interested professionals as well as with a person designated by the parent (friend, advocate, legal advisors, etc.).

The second type of IEP is the "ongoing" or "yearly review." This IEP is formulated after a special education teacher has worked with a student and has become more familiar with his strengths, weaknesses, and needs. A meeting is held to project a yearly plan designed by a team, including the special education teacher, the parent, administrative representative, any involved professional, and anyone the parent chooses to be present. This primer deals primarily with this second type of IEP.

With the advent of IDEA (PL94-142), some teachers were already following many of the required procedures. Basically, the law now requires the following steps.

1. Mainstream statement—extent to which students may participate in regular education (if appropriate)
2. Description of related services—transportation and physical education
3. Implementation dates—duration of special education and re-evaluation
4. Statement of present levels of educational performance
5. Annual goals
6. Short-term objectives
7. Objective criteria and evaluation procedures

Many teachers were routinely doing the first three of these items long before IDEA (PL94-142) existed. They are now required to address themselves to all seven items of the law plus the expanded requirements of PL101-476.

Over several years' experience, we have found that implementation is the key to solid IEPs. Chapter Six (page 47) will present an outline of how to operate an individual program once you get it on paper, as described in Chapter Four (page 23).

CHAPTER TWO

# How Do I Start?

## Assessment

States and school districts have certain options about the forms, but certain information must be included. The essential information must be:

1. Personal information
   a. Name
   b. Address
   c. Parents' names, phone, etc.
2. IEP (IDEA [PL94-142] mandated)
   a. Conference date
   b. Review date
3. Transition (PL101-476—10/90)
4. School district
   a. Building
   b. Private school
5. Grade program
   a. Identify program (LD, MR, S & ED, Gifted)
   b. Identify level (primary, elementary, one, two, three, etc.)
6. Reason for assignment
   a. Meets state criteria
   b. Narrative statement indicating reasons
7. Primary assignment
   a. Identify program (LD, MR, S & ED, Gifted)
   b. State limitations of service (e.g., specified itinerant hours, percentage of regular and special education time, etc.)
8. Projected dates
   a. Initiation dates (e.g., date of entrance in program, review date, etc.)
9. Termination dates
   a. Based on ongoing review

10. Special media materials
    a. Any special materials or devices (e.g., talking books, Braille, large print, audio tapes, typewriter, etc.)
11. Related service
    a. List any services provided in conjunction with regular education (bus transportation, physical education, speech, language, occupational therapy, physical therapy)
12. IEP team
    a. Signature of all who attend and their relationship to child

As you can see, these preceding twelve points are informational and relate to all the previous conditions for the IEP meeting. The real substance of an IEP begins with the student's present educational level (PEL).

The present educational level needs to be determined in a functional way. It is important to focus on what *can* be done as well as what *cannot* be done. It is critical to look at both strengths and weaknesses. Since the teachers will have no trouble discovering many things special children cannot do, it is important to determine strengths that can be used as a basis for instruction. The present education levels need to reflect positively on the student while giving a realistic appraisal of the needs. Some people find it easy to write a narrative that sounds good but gives few specifics. Others find it more practical to use a checklist-type insert on the IEP that identifies either the weaknesses to be worked on or conversely checks the strengths the child possesses. With the use of a checklist, one gets comprehensive coverage, and supervisors can be assured that all relevant areas are covered.

The initial determination would be, what kinds of information do you need? You must have some vehicle to check the student's current functioning level. The information will vary according to the program. For example, the programming necessary for early childhood (PL100-360), developmentally delayed, or severely retarded may need to be checked on the acquisition of social skills such as eating, dressing, and toileting. These necessary skills can be listed on a checklist, but must be broken into the smallest possible components for teaching. The checklist need not be elaborate although a commercial product like *Vineland Social Maturity Scales* or *Mann/Suiter Teacher's Handbook of Diagnostic Inventory* may be used as a base, providing you do a task analysis for each skill. You may simply want to start with a list of your own making. This should be somewhat hierarchical.

We believe checklists are efficient. It is premise based on experience. Checklists provide:

— Desired degree of coverage (brief or detailed as necessary)

— Consistency (program structure)

— Teacher guidance

A learning disabilities program can be designed with an academic emphasis, using checklists that have been developed in reading and math, and dividing these skills into their lowest teaching components. For example, we do not check all initial consonants. Instead, we check final *p*, initial *d*, and continue for every skill. Two things need to be noted: First, there are many checklists that could be used (e.g., *Walter Barbe, Fountain Valley, Brigance's Inventory of Basic Skills, Criterion Test of Basic Skills,* etc.). Our own checklists are supplied in Appendix 1 (page 74). Second, these checklists are used for initial screening for all students, and, of course, many other diagnostic instruments are used for more in-depth information when it is deemed necessary.

In our program, "how to begin" has been formulated into six steps. Following these six steps, the new teacher does not need to be overwhelmed but completes one step at a time. These six steps provide direction for a program. A new teacher working through the six steps will:

— recognize strengths and weaknesses;
— supply the sequence for individualized instruction for the student;
— provide an assessment scope;
— complete recording procedures;
— recognize the language variable.

## Step One

One math and one reading checklist per student is distributed to teachers at a late-summer in-service meeting. Teachers also receive a reading and a math assessment to be used with the checklist..

## Step Two

The teacher will begin using the assessment on the first day of classes. By a predetermined schedule, the teacher will work individually with each student for a fixed interval of 15 to 20 minutes. Unless the teacher has a specific reason to do otherwise, the teacher will begin with the reading assessment. When the reading assessment is completed, the math assignment is started.

Working 15 to 20 minutes per day on a one-to-one basis, the average reading assessment takes about a week. This varies tremendously, however, from student to student. One student may have so few skills that the reading checklist is easily completed in two sessions; others may have spotty skills and work through an entire checklist. The same follows with math. As a teacher works one-to-one assessing a student, considerable planning is required to keep others in the room occupied with meaningful tasks. The full use of an aide and audio-visual equipment can help minimize these busy first two weeks.

## Step Three

Teachers put a check on each skill item the student knows. There are no standardized ceilings, and teachers use common sense when arriving at a stopping point. For example, a student who cannot add two digits by two digits should not be tested on multiplication.

## Step Four

Checklists are divided by category. For example, a student may have a competency ceiling halfway through phonetic analysis, but the teacher would still assess word recognition and perhaps reading comprehension as other areas from which to establish base data.

## Step Five

When the assessment is completed, the *empty spaces* or unchecked items represent the student's deficits. Eventually, each unchecked skill becomes the basis for the short-term objectives.

Excerpt from Reading Checklist*

*Reading Sample:*

Final Consonant Blends (Identifies final blend from spoken word)

st __√__ ck ____ mp __√__ ld ____ nt __√__
ng __√__ nd ____ nk ____ lt ____

Initial Consonant Digraph (Identifies initial digraph from spoken word)

sh __√__ ch __√__ th ____ ph ____ wh ____

Final Consonant Digraph (Identifies final digraph from spoken word)

sh __√__ ch __√__ th ____ ph ____

*Teacher Notes:*

Needs work—phonetic

1. Final consonant blends *ck, nd, nk, ld, lt*
2. Initial consonant digraphs *th, ph, wh* (check again)
3. Final consonant digraph *th, ph*

Excerpt from Math Checklist*

*Math Sample:*

Addition: Given a printed problem, student will solve

____ One digit plus 1
__√__ One digit plus one digit
____ Commutative concept
____ Two column—no regrouping
____ Horizontal equations
____ One digit plus zero
____ Associative concept
__√__ One column addition
__√__ Two column—regrouping

Subtraction: Given printed problem, student will solve

One digit minus zero
One digit minus 1
Two digits minus one digit with regroup
Two digits minus one digit no regroup
Two digits minus one digit with regroup
Two digits minus two digits no regroup
Two digits minus two digits with regroup
Three digits with regroup
Horizontal Equation

* The entire Reading and Math Checklists will be found in Appendix One.

*Teacher Notes:*

Needs work—addition/subtraction

1. Addition

   One digit plus zero
   Associative concept
   Commutative concept
   Horizontal equations
   Two column regrouping

2. Subtraction

   Two digits minus one digit no regroup
   Two digits minus one digit with regroup
   Two digits minus two digits no regroup
   Two digits minus two digits with regroup
   Three digits with regroup
   Horizontal equation

## Step Six

At this time, start your collection of data on language needs. Much data can be accumulated through teacher observation. For example, (1) does the student speak in sentences; (2) is the syntax correct; (3) how much information can the student put on a 3x5 card: his name, address, etc.; (4) mechanics; (5) production of written language; (6) creative writing. The teacher's judgment should point toward:

1. *TOWL (Test of Written Language)*
2. *The Carrow Elicited Language Inventory for Syntax*
3. *Mann/Suiter Teacher's Handbook of Diagnostic Screening for Language*
4. *Cooper/School Language Inventory for Teachers Checklist*

## Other Considerations

Depending on your program needs, perceptual information may be desired. You will need sensory data about visual, auditory, or motor impairment that interferes with learning, as well as identifying the dominant, preferred mode of the student. Many psychologists recommend or use:

1. *Wepman Test of Auditory Discrimination*
2. *Lindamood Auditory Conceptualization Test*
3. *Detroit Tests of Learning Aptitude* (auditory-visual)
4. *Rosner* (auditory-visual)
5. *Illinois Test of Psycholinguistic Abilities, Revised* (auditory-visual)
6. *The Ayres Space Test*

(This perceptual research is still considered valid and useful by many educators for early intervention children even though the research data was collected in the 60's.)

For some students, *special skills* may be a prime area of concern. Information from behavior rating scales should be examined. Testimony from teachers and parents should be solicited. A checklist could be constructed. In essence, if social skills are to be included in the IEP, a basis for skill selection must be laid down through a data base.

The move toward early intervention, which is already in place in some states, will need the same kind of approach as the transition and post school plans if they are implemented in the public school sector. At this time, it is not clear where the early intervention will be conducted. For example, in our state, this intervention may be conducted through preschool agencies. Once the determination is made, teachers in states that elect to conduct this program in the public schools may need to be trained. Clearly, the personnel responsible for early intervention will need professional training in childhood development. Theoretically, IEPs for preschoolers would have developmental goals including language development, social goals, physical development, speech and behavior. We believe the general model could be adapted for these IEPs by using the developmental checklist currently in existence.

In summary, our model was developed to address basic skill needs in a school setting. We are convinced that the expanded and changing needs in special education are a challenge to educators. We also are convinced that the model we developed can be generalized to meet these expanding needs by substituting checklists of required curriculum.

Currently, the move toward early intervention is accelerating. Some states are already acting on mandates while other are slowly moving in that direction. PL99-257, an educational component known as high risk pre-school, now requires intensive work on developing an appropriate curriculum. Clearly the curriculum will be developmental with specific attention to:

1. Physical development, which includes but is not limited to gross motor, fine motor, and visual skills
2. Cognitive development
3. Language and speech development, which should include an assessment of the child's auditory skills
4. Psycho-social development
5. Self-help skills

Two standardized tests used in our locality are:

1. *Vineland Adaptive Behavior Scale*
2. *Bayley Scales of Infant Development Mental Scale*

There are a variety of tests used in other areas that will work as well.

As programs are developed locally as per the law, criteria will be established. From state/local criteria, checklists and curricula should follow. Since a current mandate is in progress, no recommendations can be made until local agencies develop inter-agency programs.

The model explained in this book can be applied to early intervention IEPs.

In a similar manner vocational IEPs can be developed and coordinated with the local curriculum. Many vocational programs already are operating competency-based checklists. It would not be difficult to transform a competency-based checklist into an assessment that would generate an IEP. Some task analysis may be required as noted in Step Five (page 13). The process of using a yes/no check system that works for consonant clusters would just as easily apply to specific vocational competencies.

## Summary

Once the basic concept is learned from this book, you can transfer the model of how to develop an IEP that is consistent, efficient, and organized. This model is basically a four step procedure:

1. Acquire or design a relevant assessment.
2. Transform current data into a checklist format with yes/no answers.
3. Administer that assessment.
4. Use the no column as the basis for your IEP.

Most of the *Primer* uses basic skills as an example because that is the program on which the model was developed. However, whatever the specific or unique curriculum needs are, they can be used with the model.

CHAPTER THREE

# Conducting the IEP Meeting

The IEP meeting should be attended by as many people as have a genuine interest in the child. Parents legally have the right to bring whomever they wish; and certain cases may call for several professionals, such as psychologist, social worker, physical therapist, etc. For most parent conferences, however, the most proficient, productive meetings will be a minimum group consisting of teacher, parents, and special education specialist. Unless there is a real need for other professional input, the larger group lacks efficiency.

The individual presiding at the meeting should make the opening introductions and put others at ease. It would seem in most cases that it would be better psychology to seat parents and teachers in adjacent positions so the teacher can present data to the parents. When the teacher sits on the opposite side of the desk, she erects an unnecessary psychological barrier to communication. The administrator in charge should be seated near enough to interact with other participants. The administrator should open the meeting by outlining the purpose of the meeting, and it is suggested that the law itself be cited in connection with the purpose.

The next step is to present the current functioning level of the student to the LEA (local education agency) team. Not only should test scores be given, but also the specifics that indicate what the student can or cannot do should be presented. In some cases, the best policy is to provide parents with evaluation data and a full explanation of what the student was able to do, as well as what he could not do. Some teachers may question the efficacy of this procedure, but our own experience has shown that people are more supportive of recommendations once they have seen the results. This also adds validity to the conference since it includes the parents in the basic operation (evaluation).

It is important to keep the focus of the conference on the strengths and weaknesses of the child; and, though relevant anecdotal material may be welcome, it is important not to allow digressions about history or anecdotes or other family matters to intrude on the real purpose of the conference. The teacher needs to keep focusing on the data and will find that offering and pointing to the checklists tends to keep the meeting on course. One of the pitfalls to avoid during the conference is free-ranging discussion of such topics as:

1. Last year's teacher
2. Previous professional shortcomings

3. Sibling problems
4. Sibling successes (parents will frequently want to note that the other children are successful)
5. Nonproductive conversation concerning etiology
6. Other irrelevant areas of social conversation

When parents start on the above subjects, the teacher is wise to refocus the conference by looking down at the checklist or test data and returning to it. In the interest of flexibility, an administrator needs to be very careful about screening, and rather skillful at sorting relevant and irrelevant data. This may require some listening at first. Once the administrator is convinced that the remarks are in no way related to the subject at hand, however, firmness may be required. In that case, the administrator might lean across the table, saying one of the following:

1. This is not relevant in today's meeting.
2. We are not in a position to comment on that subject.
3. It must be very rewarding to be getting your problems solved.
4. That is a good subject for another meeting if you feel strongly on the issue.

By contrast, it is important to solicit parental input that is relevant to the educational program, and certainly there should be every indication that we are genuinely interested in the student.

Some parents will come in with notes, suggestions, and questions. Most others will not be that prepared, and it is important to draw them out so they have contributed to the conference and will support the program. The following are some questions you might want to ask to elicit relevant information.

1. What kinds of things does your child do at home?
   a. Look for peer interaction
   b. Behavior problem
   c. Organized home life
   d. Sibling interaction
2. How much TV does he watch?
   a. What programs does the child watch (e.g., violence, cartoons, late movies)?
   b. How much parent attention does the child get?
   c. Is there evening structure (e.g,. regular meals, bedtimes)?
3. What are his hobbies?
   a. Can the child perform fine-motor activities (e.g., model cars, craft projects)?

## Alternatives

An alternative to behavioral objectives, which focus on what the child eventually will do, is a teacher objective, which focuses on what the teacher will do. For example:

1. Teacher will review . . . .
2. Teacher will reteach . . . .
3. Teacher will teach . . . .
4. Teacher will combine with . . . .
5. Teacher will introduce . . . .
6. Teacher will drill.

Note: Sometimes this approach is more realistic in special education. Experience shows that special students often need to be retaught the same material over which they have previously shown mastery. The preceding descriptions may be a more accurate approach than describing students' actions since teacher behaviors can be described with some accuracy, and exceptional children's behaviors may not be predicted dependably.

## Data Needed

As summarized from Chapter Two, statistical information mandated for an IEP is as follows:

1. Name
2. Address
3. Birthdate
4. Phone
5. Parents' names
6. Date of IEP conference
7. Date of review
8. Reason for assignment
9. Names of team members
10. Related services
11. Summary of current educational functions

The current functioning level is the sum of the child's strengths and weaknesses and should include current achievement data—for example, test scores from any current achievement test the child may be given in addition to specific skill information that the regular teacher supplies through testimony or current work sample. For example:

> Johnny is reading at 2.4 level, according to the *Wide Range Achievement Test.* He tends to guess at words he doesn't know and frequently confuses common sight words, especially the sight words *house, horse, was,* and *saw.* His comprehension is very poor, and he is unable to extract information through reading or to summarize information.

You may also choose to direct attention to selected information from the psychological evaluation. Without in any way discussing the psychological scores, you may find it useful to extract some perceptual strengths or weaknesses. Many psychologists include information relevant to academic functioning, but be careful about using the functioning levels if the psychological assessment is more than a year old. For example, psychologists frequently comment on the auditory, visual, or language functioning of a child. This information can be summarized and incorporated into the current functioning level of the IEP. Too much information might be overwhelming, particularly if remediation has not yet been planned.

The balance of the IEP may be one page—or thirty. It involves the total projected instructional program that was agreed upon at the conference. Usually, the IEP encompasses one or more subject areas: reading, math, spelling, and language, in addition to any special arrangement such as occupational therapy or speech. IEPs are also written to cover modification of the regular education curriculum. Such modifications may include but are not limited to assignment reduction, special taping, an assigned reading, an alternative assignment, or a behavioral contact. When these modifications require special effort on the part of regular education teachers, input is doubly necessary. Most frequently, a modified program requires both regular teacher and special teacher to implement it (for example, reading of a test in a given content area). Broadly stated long-range goals encompass a general area of instruction (e.g., phonetic analysis) and state the expected functional endpoint of the teaching process with respect to student gains.

The third component lists short-range objectives that are more specific and more liable to teacher accountability. Considerable thought should be given to their formulation since these are the goals the teacher will answer for at the IEP review date.

For convenience, some suggested goals and objectives have been included on the reading and math checklists. These objectives are stated in behavioral terms and are very skill-specific.

The academic checklists provided in this primer can be used with any individualized program that teaches reading or math (e.g., learning disabilities, educable mentally retarded, gifted, regular education).

## Transition

At the IEP conference, before the student's 16th birthday, the teacher must discuss how the transition from school to work will be planned.

Each state has criteria and professional involvement procedures that must be implemented. The parent's and student's interests, needs and aptitudes are a key component to this plan. The teacher and guidance counselor should be prepared with aptitude testing results to discuss a realistic plan. Outside professionals must be invited to this meeting.

This list is a suggestion of professionals that could be involved: vocational education counselors, community college or university representatives, agency staff (Office of Mental Health, Office of Social Programs, Department of Public Welfare, Office of Mental Retardation).

## When Agreement Isn't Reached

There will be times when the parent is not satisfied and refuses to accept the IEP. At that point, the conference can simply be ended. However, this is not a positive ending, and the following is a strategy that the administrator chairing the conference might try. Ask the parents to go through and mark all the objectives with which they agree and conversely to note the objectives with which they disagree. Next, ask them to write the objectives that they feel are missing. At this point, the administrator can quickly define the area of disagreement. In all probability, it will be very narrow. Experience shows that a skillful administrator can arbitrate such situations with a little tact. However, it should be noted that teacher and administrator should not agree with IEP goals that are totally impossible or not relevant. "Peace at any price" simply creates problems down the line. If the program is to be credible, goals must be attainable and reasonable. Most parents are reasonable when the conference is handled with skill and tact. Keep in mind that parents really want what is best for the child, and once they have had their say, they are able to compromise if they trust the professionals involved.

CHAPTER FOUR

# Writing the Finished Product

IEP forms in most states are similar since general requirements are mandated by IDEA (PL94-142). If you have a choice of forms, several samples can be found beginning on page 91.

The IEP is usually written in behavioral terms. Behavioral terms traditionally focus on the child. The emphasis is on the observable behavior the student demonstrates after instruction. To be a true behavioral objective, both condition and criteria are included. There is considerable emphasis on the verb that is used. Selecting the verb is important since it tells exactly what you will observe the child doing on completion of the task. The condition states what the student is expected to do and the criteria states specifically how accurate the student must be before he has achieved the task as specified. You will note that the behavioral objectives used on the checklists are set up in traditional "ABC" order. However, since many forms in use provide a column for the condition (evaluation) and another column called criteria (criteria), some teachers omit the condition and criteria in the long-range goal to avoid excessive writing.

You may choose to include the entire long-range goal or use the abbreviated form by omitting the optional portions that are parenthesized.

The following are a list of *acceptable* behavioral terms, followed by a list of unacceptable behavioral terms.

**Acceptable Descriptive Terms for Writing Objectives**

| | | | |
|---|---|---|---|
| Add | Discriminate | Match | Repeat |
| Analyze | Divide | Multiply | Review |
| Answer | Edit | Name aloud | Say |
| Choose | Explain | Organize | Sit |
| Circle | Find | Place | Solve |
| Complete | Identify | Point | Spell |
| Construct | Include | Proofread | Subtract |
| Correctly identify | Listen | Prove | Underline |
| Define | List in writing | Read | Use |
| Describe | Make | Repair | Write |

**Unacceptable Terms**

| | |
|---|---|
| Know | Demonstrate the ability to |
| Understand | Think |
| Learn | Be able to |
| | Can |

## Writing the Agreed-Upon Goals

At this point, the teacher starts writing the IEP. The long-range goals would generally be in one or more of the following areas:

1. Phonetic analysis
2. Reading comprehension
3. Study habits
4. Math computation
5. Sets
6. Measuring
7. Simple sentence structure
8. Vocabulary expansion
9. Categories
10. Auditory sequencing

These major goals should be set up in behavioral terms (Appendix One) and should include the vehicle used to evaluate and the criteria expected.

## Get Your Checklist

Working from your checklist, look at your long-range goals at the top of each grouping. Copy your long-range goal from the checklist to the appropriate space on your IEP form.

Next, list your short-term goals with as much specificity as you deem necessary.

Note: In the evaluation column there is a one-to-one correspondence between short-range objectives and items. This means that for every short-term objective, you must declare what you will use to evaluate the student on that objective.

It is important that this column be realistic. Unless the material for testing is at hand, testing may not take place as frequently as it should. When the teacher has to travel for a specific test or make special arrangements, there may be a tendency to avoid the obvious.

## INDIVIDUALIZED EDUCATION PROGRAM

ID# ____________

INTAKE IEP    REVISED IEP

Student Name: David Barclay

DOB 2/7/84    Sex: (M) or F    Grade 4

IEP Conference Date 9/20/92

PL 89-313    Y: 1 2 3 OR (N)

IEP Implementation Date 9/21/92

MDE Date 7/15/91

IEP Review/Revision Date 9/21/93

NORA Date 9/21/92

Referral Date 10/15/89

Parent Name: Mr. & Mrs. Joseph Barclay

Parent District Norris School District

Address 426 Main Street

Norris, PA

Student District Norris School District

District of Class or Service Norris School District

Phone (212) 893-9641

School Building Norris Elementary

Teacher of Class Ms. Norma Malik

| Type of Service (mark all that apply) | | Level of Intervention | % of time | Service Provider | Initiation Date | Anticipated Duration |
|---|---|---|---|---|---|---|
| Academic gifted support | | | | | | |
| Academic learning support | X | Resource Room | 50% | Learning Specialist | 9/21/92 | 9/21/93 |
| Life skills support | | | | | | |
| Emotional support | | | | | | |
| Deaf or Hearing Impaired sensory support | | | | | | |
| Blind or Vision Impaired sensory support | | | | | | |
| Speech & Language support* | | | | | | |
| Physical support | | | | | | |
| Autistic support | | | | | | |
| Multihandicapped support | | | | | | |

*AIU SP-L
TYPE _____ SEVERITY _____ YEARS _____

Tot. % Time Receiving Sp. Ed. 50%

Tot. % Time Receiving Reg. Ed. 50%

### IEP PLANNING MEMBERS

| NAME | TITLE |
|---|---|
| | PARENT |
| | TEACHER |
| | SUPERVISOR |
| | DISTRICT REPRESENTATIVE |
| | |
| | |

* Page one of IEP form used by Allegheny Intermediate Unit.

Dear ______________________________,

In order to comply with the state requirements listed in IDEA (PL94-142), it is necessary to write an IEP for each child who has met the criteria for special education classes. The law requires the parents to have an active part in writing their child's program; therefore, conferences will be held for this purpose.

A recent memo stated that it is necessary to have notes from regular classroom teachers relevant to integration of modification in regular education (e.g., [a] student is integrated into regular fifth grade science curriculum; or [b] student is integrated in social studies but all tests will be given orally).

For your convenience, please fill out the following checklist for the students for whom you are responsible. They will be used at the conference and kept in the student's educational file.

Thank You.

______________________________

---

Name ______________________________________________ Date______________

______________________ (is integrated, audits—no grade given) on the ______________ grade level in the area of ______________________________. The following methods are being used to aid in the learning process and allow for individual differences in the regular classroom.

______ Communication with special class teacher to provide reinforcement

______ Oral tests because of motor difficulties

______ Special seating to lessen distractibility

______ Simplified worksheets

______ Individual explanations of directions

______ Taping of reading material

______ Outlining of text chapters for inportant points

______ Homework assignments written on board to be copied or on handout to allow for language and memory difficulties

______ Reduced assignments

______ Identification of two or three key concepts required to pass units

Please add any other suggestions that you have found helpful.

______ Calculator

______ Open book test

______ Lesson organizer

______ Structural study guide

______ Key words and definitions

______ Multiple choice questions

______ Highlighted textbook of key concepts

______ Word bank of key vocabulary

---

Date ____________________.

Addendum for ____________________________ IEP

of ______________________________

The special modifications and adaptations that are made for the student in order for him or her to participate in the basic education programs of social studies and science at the ________ grade level are as follows:

I. General:

1. The student is in a regular homeroom which lends itself for his participation with his peers for daily activities, such as lunch, and classes for art, music, P.E., and library.
2. Ability grouping—The student is placed in the ____________ group so that instruction does not take a fast pace, so that instruction can be presented in short segments, and so students are not required to produce an amount that is unrealistic if not frustrating.

II. Specific:

| | |
|---|---|
| 1. Grades | Unofficial grades are kept of the student to eliminate the pressure of working for a grade. |
| 2. Tests | Tests are read to the student. |
| 3. Notes | Instructor's notes are thermofaxed for the student so he does not have to copy notes. |
| 4. Oral reading in class | The student is called on to read only if he volunteers. |
| 5. Special projects | The student is encouraged to do special projects in these subject areas for extra credit and release of pressure when the requirements are too demanding. |

## Suggested Accommodations

### Classroom

1. Preferred seating
2. Behavior modification techniques
3. Good progress reports
4. Peer reinforcement

### Instructional Areas

1. Taped instructional lessons
2. Assigned project for additional credit
3. Individualized study skill sheets
4. Peer tutoring
5. Audiovisual aid
6. Adaptive homework assignments
7. Modification of text
8. Learning centers
9. Resource room support
10. Class assignments
11. Compensation notebook
12. Credit for class participation

### Tests

1. Oral test with instructor
2. Oral test with resource teacher
3. Taped tests
4. Adapted tests—objective and essay
5. Make-up tests
6. All tests completed in resource room
7. Open book test
8. Matching test
9. Multiple choice test
10. True/false test

## Case History Number 1—Bob

Bob has been in the learning disabilities program for four years and is currently in a junior high school program. Last year, Bob was on the honor roll in junior high. His psychological reevaluation was scatter ranging from 1 in Coding to 19 in Object Assembly on the *Wechsler Intelligence Scale for Children—Revised* (WISC-R). Every learning disabilities teacher he has had has stated that his average IQ score is a low estimate of his ability.

Bob is a *nonreader.* He scores 3.1 on the *Wide Range Achievement Test* (WRAT) Reading score, but this can be attributed to intense effort over four years, and although Bob can do competent work with phonic exercises in isolation, there is little carry-over or generalization to reading. All of Bob's work is taped for him since he learns well auditorially. He is well liked by teachers in the building, who state he participates eagerly in class and fulfills all assignments. Bob frequently volunteers for extra projects to raise his class grade.

Learning disabilities teachers report that Bob will work with any material if you tell him it will help him learn to read. He is not "insulted" by "baby exercises," nor does he balk at doing work over and over again. Asked what his biggest wish is, he will reply, "Learn to read."

Aside from the regular learning disabilities program, for several months Bob has been a participant in a federal project in association with the local university, in which intensive remedial reading work was attempted. Bob worked very hard but little progress was noted.

The psychological report emphasized the low arithmetic ability, but math has never been the problem to Bob that reading has been. His WRAT score of 4.2 is probably an accurate measure of his ability under pressure, but Bob has been able to hold his own in math if he has problems read to him and is given unlimited time to check his computations. He is able to do metric conversions and is functional with general arithmetic (addition, subtraction, multiplication, division, averaging, graphs, and some fractions.

Any written language work is extremely difficult for Bob—which is not surprising, since reading precedes writing in hierarchy of language.

Should you meet Bob, you would automatically note what a neat, bright, verbal young man he is. He would be at ease conversing with you and is equally at ease with his peer group. There is nothing in his demeanor or interaction that would not be typical of any junior high school student. Bob's honor roll status is not "charity," but a true reflection of his effort and achievement with fully acknowledged learning disabilities class support.

In summary, Bob is a four-year veteran of the learning disabilities program. Despite extraordinary measures by both Bob and several teachers, he still cannot read effectively. His honor roll status attests to his general learning ability. At 14 years of age, Bob has not "grown out" of his perceptual problems but has learned some valuable survival skills.

Instruction Area: Reading | Student's Name: Bob | School Year

Annual Goal: Bob will improve in his ability to sound out words.

*Short-Term Objective*

| *Educational Tasks* | *Evaluation Procedures/Conditions* | *Success Criteria* | *Progress* |
|---|---|---|---|
| Bob will break words apart into syllables or little words when sounding out new or unknown words. | Teacher observation of Bob's oral reading | Consistent improvement of sounding out words | |
| Bob will use phonic elements to sound out new or unknown words. | Teacher observation of Bob's oral reading | Consistent improvement of sounding out words | |

Instructional Area: English | Student's Name: Bob | School Year

Annual Goal: Bob will improve in his written expression.

*Short-Term Objective*

| *Educational Tasks* | *Evaluation Procedures/Conditions* | *Success Criteria* | *Progress* |
|---|---|---|---|
| Bob will write complete sentences with proper capitalization and punctuation | Unit texts and worksheets | 80% by the end of the year | |
| Bob will write grammatically correct sentences | Teacher analysis of written work | Consistent improvement in performance | |

Instructional Area: Math | Student's Name: Bob | School Year

Annual Goal: Bob will attend the eighth-grade math class with the following modifications.

*Short-Term Objective*

| *Educational Tasks* | *Evaluation Procedures/Conditions* | *Success Criteria* | *Progress* |
|---|---|---|---|
| In the Resource Room Bob will have reinforcement worksheets that coincide with the math class. | Evaluation procedure will be determined by the eighth grade math teacher | Criteria of success will be determined by the eighth grade math teacher | |

Instruction Area: Social Studies | Student's Name: Bob | School Year

Annual Goal: Bob will attend the eighth-grade social studies class with the following modifications.

*Short-Term Objective*

| *Educational Tasks* | *Evaluation Procedures/Conditions* | *Success Criteria* | *Progress* |
|---|---|---|---|
| In the Resource Room Bob will have all social studies terms identified orally. | Evaluation procedure will be determined by the eighth grade social studies teacher. | Criteria of success will be determined by the eighth-grade social studies teacher. | |
| In the Resource Room Bob will have reinforcement on all Social Studies maps and locations. | | | |

Instructional Area: Reading | Student's Name: Bob | School Year

Annual Goal: Bob will improve in his ability to comprehend material text.

*Short-Term Objective*

| *Educational Tasks* | *Evaluation Procedures/Conditions* | *Success Criteria* | *Progress* |
|---|---|---|---|
| 1. Bob will use context signs in figuring out meanings of unfamiliar words. | 1. Specific skill series—last 2 pages in "Using the Context," "Drawing Conclusions," and "Getting the Main Idea." | 1. 80% accuracy | |
| 2. Bob will draw conclusions from material he has read. | 2. Specific skill series—last 2 pages in "Using the Context," "Drawing Conclusions," and "Getting the Main Idea." | 2. 80% accuracy | |

Instructional Area: Reading (cont.) | Student's Name: Bob | School Year

Annual Goal: Bob will improve in his ability to comprehend material text.

*Short-Term Objective*

| *Educational Tasks* | *Evaluation Procedures/Conditions* | *Success Criteria* | *Progress* |
|---|---|---|---|
| 3. Bob will tell the main idea of a passage he has read. | 3. Specific skill series—last 2 pages in "Using the Context," "Drawing Conclusions," and "Getting the Main Idea." | 3. 80% accuracy | |

Instructional Area: Academic subjects | Student's Name: Bob | School Year

Annual Goal: Bob will participate in a regular tenth-grade program.

*Short-Term Objective*

| *Educational Tasks* | *Evaluation Procedures/Conditions* | *Success Criteria* | *Progress* |
|---|---|---|---|
| Will provide back-up tutoring and reinforcement in the following academic subjects when requested throughout the year math, science, social studies, and language. | Regular education<br>Teacher evaluation | Regular education with tests. | |

Instructional Area: Reading | Student's Name: Bob | School Year

Annual Goal: Bob will prove competent at oral reading while utilizing the following skills.

*Short-Term Objective*

| *Educational Tasks* | *Evaluation Procedures/Conditions* | *Success Criteria* | *Progress* |
|---|---|---|---|
| Bob will read 80% of words correctly (at appropriate level). | Reading paragraphs orally to teacher | 80% accuracy | |
| Bob will use correct phrasing. | Reading paragraphs orally to teacher | 80% accuracy | |
| Bob will react to punctuation. | Reading paragraphs orally to teacher | 80% accuracy | |
| Bob will read with expression. | Reading paragraphs orally to teacher | 80% accuracy | |
| Bob will read clearly and distinctly. | Reading paragraphs orally to teacher | 80% accuracy | |
| Bob will read fluently. | Reading paragraphs orally to teacher | 80% accuracy | |

Instructional Area: Language | Student's Name: Bob | School Year

Annual Goal: Bob will develop functional receptive/interpretive language skills.

| | *Educational Tasks* | *Evaluation Procedures/Conditions* | *Success Criteria* | *Progress* |
|---|---|---|---|---|
| *Short-Term Objective* | Bob will retell a story in his own words that has been read to him. | Teacher directed oral evaluation | 80% accuracy | |
| | Bob will answer questions (factual, inferential). | Teacher directed oral evaluation | 80% accuracy | |
| | Bob will identify nonsense ideas presented orally in a story. | Teacher directed oral evaluation | 80% accuracy | |
| | Bob will choose the meaning of orally presented vocabulary. | Teacher directed oral evaluation | 80% accuracy | |

Instructional Area: Language | Student's Name: Bob | School Year

Annual Goal: Bob will develop functional written language skills.

| | *Educational Tasks* | *Evaluation Procedures/Conditions* | *Success Criteria* | *Progress* |
|---|---|---|---|---|
| *Short-Term Objective* | Bob will use correct spelling. | Teacher made worksheet | 80% accuracy | |
| | Bob will use correct word order in sentence formation. | Teacher made worksheet | 100% accuracy | |
| | Bob will write sentences of the declaration, imperative, interrogative, and exclamatory type. | Teacher made worksheet | Proofed samples | |
| | Bob will use appropriate capitalization. | Teacher made worksheet | 100% accuracy | |
| | Bob will use appropriate punctuation of all types in writing. | Teacher made worksheet | 80% accuracy | |
| | Bob will use all parts of speech correctly. (Noun, verb, adverb, adjective, pronoun, conjunction, preposition, and interjection) | Teacher made worksheet | Correct speech patterns | |

## Case History Number 2—Tara

Tara is a new student who has recently been accepted into the learning disabilities program. While she is still based with her first-grade peers, it has been obvious since kindergarten that Tara is significantly below her peers in perceptual development and academic readiness. For example, Tara still can neither identify or produce a rhyme, despite extensive kindergarten effort with nursery rhymes and jingles. Tara also fails to discriminate auditorially at the level she needs for prereading and initial reading skills. It has been noted that her gross auditory skills are good, receptive language is adequate, and expressive language is close to average when compared to her classmates.

An effort to start "writing" (printing) has been delayed because of visual immaturity. Tara can neither color nor cut. A visual examination was not so helpful as expected. The optometrist found a slight ambliopic condition, on which he was working with some visual exercises, but he was unable to make a prediction of binocular competence for Tara by the ensuing school year.

While there was extreme failure in reading, arithmetic has emerged as a comparative success for Tara. Actually, math, too, is behind but much less so. There has been a one-to-one correspondence developed, and Tara can "rattle-off" her numbers. Like reading, it is not clear that the sound-to-symbol relationship has been established. Records would indicate that Tara is ready for basic computations.

It is recommended that remediation begin with pre-academic (perceptual) skills combined with basic reading, math, and language skills. As much integration as possible between academic and perceptual needs should be attempted so Tara does not fall further behind her peers.

A list of needs:

1. Math: Not bad. Ready to start computations.
2. Visual: Lacks hand/eye coordination. Needs exercises.
3. Spatial: Needs to be taught about space, time, and money.
4. Auditory: Lacks discrimination. Does not have sound-to-symbol concept firmly established. Needs instruction in following directions and blending.
5. Reading and writing must be started at the readiness level.

Instructional Area: Perception | Student's Name: Tara | School Year

Annual Goal: Tara will improve competency in the following areas of auditory perception.

*Short-Term Objective*

| *Educational Tasks* | *Evaluation Procedures/Conditions* | *Success Criteria* | *Progress* |
|---|---|---|---|
| Tara will improve in auditory discrimination of vowels and rhyming families. | First Practice Book, Sounds & Words<br>A. D. D. program tests | 100% | |
| Tara's auditory memory will improve for sentences and reorganization. | Slingerland C tests | 100% | |
| Tara's ability to choose words when individual sounds are given will improve. | M. W. M. program auditory closure workbooks | 80% | |
| Tara's ability to blend 3, 4, 5 sounds together to form words will improve | A. D. D. program auditory blending workbooks | 90% | |

Instructional Area: Perception | Student's Name: Tara | School Year

Annual Goal: Given a teacher-made worksheet, Tara will prove competent on Directionality and Body Image Concepts.

*Short-Term Objective*

| *Educational Tasks* | *Evaluation Procedures/Conditions* | *Success Criteria* | *Progress* |
|---|---|---|---|
| Tara will recognize left-right in her body, in space, and generalized to paper. | Teacher-made cassette skills | 100% | |

Instructional Area: Math | Student's Name: Tara | School Year

Annual Goal: Tara will improve basic Computation Skills

| Short-Term Objective: *Educational Tasks* | *Evaluation Procedures* | *Success Criteria* | *Progress* |
|---|---|---|---|
| Tara will master addition facts from 1 to 20. | Given a Stern Math worksheet and a set of Stern Blocks | 90% | |
| Tara will master subtraction facts from 1-10. | Given a Stern Math worksheet and a set of Stern Blocks | 90% | |
| Tara will do 2-digit by 2-digit math addition on a traditional drill sheet with no regrouping. | Given a master's test from a traditional math program | 90% | |

Instructional Area: Perception | Student's Name: Tara | School Year

Annual Goal: Tara will improve competency in the following areas of visual perception.

| Short-Term Objective: *Educational Tasks* | *Evaluation Procedures/Conditions* | *Success Criteria* | *Progress* |
|---|---|---|---|
| Tara will improve in visual discrimination of words. | Remedial reading dittoes (word shapes) configuration box tests | 100% | |
| Tara will improve in form consistency. | Frostig tests finding words on check-board in basal reading series | 100% | |
| Tara will improve in position-in-space concepts. | Use of Frostig tests. | 100% | |
| Tara will improve in spatial relations. | Frostig tests; parquetry design tests | 80% | |

Instructional Area: Reading    Student's Name: Tara    School Year

Annual Goal: Tara will increase phonic analysis skills.

*Short-Term Objective*

| *Educational Tasks* | *Evaluation Procedures/Conditions* | *Success Criteria* | *Progress* |
|---|---|---|---|
| Will identify and reproduce initial consonant blends. | Commercial worksheet, tape recorder. | 90% accuracy on 3 trials | |
| Will identify and reproduce short vowel sounds. | A. D. D.; teacher worksheets; vowel wheels. | 85% accuracy on daily trials in 1 week | |
| Will identify and reproduce long vowel sounds. | A. D. D.; teacher worksheets; vowel wheels. | 85% accuracy on daily trials in 1 week | |
| Will identify hard and soft letters. | Teacher observation; teacher worksheet | 85% accuracy on 2 trials | |

Instructional Area: Reading    Student's Name: Tara    School Year

Annual Goal: Tara will increase primary structural analysis skills.

*Short-Term Objective*

| *Educational Tasks* | *Evaluation Procedures/Conditions* | *Success Criteria* | *Progress* |
|---|---|---|---|
| Will identify and produce rhyming families. | Teacher worksheets | 85% accuracy on 2 trials | |
| Will convert *y* to *i* plus ending in nouns and verbs. | Commercial worksheet teacher observation | 85% accuracy on 3 trials | |
| Will identify and reproduce contractions. | Commercial worksheets; tape recorder | 85% accuracy on 3 trials | |

*Short-Term Objective*

Instructional Area: Reading | Student's Name: Tara | School Year

Annual Goal: Tara will increase word recognition skills.

| *Educational Tasks* | *Evaluation Procedures/Conditions* | *Success Criteria* | *Progress* |
|---|---|---|---|
| Will say first-grade words. | *Scott Foresman Hide & Seek* | 100% accuracy on 1 trial | |
| Will say first half of second-grade words. | *Scott Foresman Hide & Seek* | 100% accuracy on 1 trial | |

*Short-Term Objective*

Instructional Area: Reading | Student's Name: Tara | School Year

Annual Goal: Tara will improve oral comprehension skills on level two.

| *Educational Tasks* | *Evaluation Procedures/Conditions* | *Success Criteria* | *Progress* |
|---|---|---|---|
| Will use titles and page numbers. | Teacher observation | 85% accuracy | |
| Will use proper phrasing and voice inflection while reading. | Teacher observation; tape recorder | 85% accuracy | |
| Will find the main idea. | Teacher observation | 85% accuracy on 5 trials | |

Instructional Area: Mathematics | Student's Name: Tara | School Year

Annual Goal: Tara will improve computation skills.

Short-Term Objective

| Educational Tasks | Evaluation Procedures/Conditions | Success Criteria | Progress |
|---|---|---|---|
| Will write and give orally addition and subtraction facts form 1-18 | Teacher observation; Language Master | 90% accuracy on 2 trials | |
| Will compute 2 column regrouping in addition and subtraction. | Teacher worksheet | 85% accuracy on 3 trials | |
| Will compute 2 digit minus 1 digit re-grouping. | Teacher worksheet commercial worksheet | 85% accuracy on 3 trials | |
| Will compute 2 digit plus 1 digit re-grouping. | Teacher worksheet commercial worksheet | 85% accuracy on 3 trials | |
| Will use the expanded form of numbers. | Teacher observation; teacher worksheet | 85% accuracy on 2 trials | |

Instructional Area: Mathematics | Student's Name: Tara | School Year

Annual Goal: Tara will improve number sequencing skills.

Short-Term Objective

| Educational Tasks | Evaluation Procedures/Conditions | Success Criteria | Progress |
|---|---|---|---|
| Will copy and organize numbers in a given space. | Teacher observation | 90% accuracy on 2 trials | |
| Will recognize and complete patterns. | Teacher worksheets | 85% accuracy on 3 trials | |
| Will arrange numbers from smallest to largest. | Teacher worksheets | 90% accuracy on 2 trials | |

Short-Term Objective

Instructional Area: Reading | Student's Name: Tara | School Year

Annual Goal: Tara will improve silent comprehension skills on level two.

| *Educational Tasks* | *Evaluation Procedures/Conditions* | *Success Criteria* | *Progress* |
|---|---|---|---|
| Will follow directions. | Teacher observation | 85% accuracy on 3 trials | |
| Will recall what has been read silently. | Teacher observation | 85% accuracy on 3 trials | |

Short-Term Objective

Instructional Area: Language Arts | Student's Name: Tara | School Year

Annual Goal: Tara will improve grammar skills.

| *Educational Tasks* | *Evaluation Procedures/Conditions* | *Success Criteria* | *Progress* |
|---|---|---|---|
| Will utilize capitalization rules. | Commercial worksheet | 85% accuracy on 3 trials | |
| Will define and use properly the parts of speech: noun, verb, adjective | Teacher observation; teacher worksheet | 85% accuracy on 3 trials | |
| Will identify and supply antonyms. | Tape recorder; teacher worksheet | 90% accuracy on 2 trials | |

CHAPTER FIVE

# The Placement Conference

Once a student has been approved for placement, it is the administrator's duty to organize the staff and formulate plans for the final placement. It will be necessary for the administrator to preside at the meetings. These tasks must be done by a member of the administrative staff and may not be handled by conveniently available or other interested personnel, such as counselors or social workers. Although all these people may be involved in the LEA team, the administrator needs to:

1. Send a form letter to the parent advising of the meeting.
2. Instruct the teacher to begin collecting assessment information (checklists) as covered in Chapter Two.
3. Instruct the support personnel to collect relevant data.
4. In conjunction with the principal's wishes, establish the time and place of the meeting.
5. Notify all of the members of the LEA team.
6. Arrange for a substitute or alternate coverage for staff members attending the meeting.
7. Just prior to the meeting, check that the teacher has completed all required information.
8. Review regulations and pages of this manual.

## Supportive Service

A lesson of supportive service is indigenous to the concept of least restrictive environment (LRE). Just how much supportive service will be needed, and who will supply this service is a question that must be addressed in the IEP meeting.

An example of supportive service:

1. Does the student need adaptive physical education?
2. Will special transportation be necessary?
3. Can the student tolerate a home room with his peers?
4. How much integration can the student participate in (e.g., some, very little, none)?

5. Will any special audio-visual equipment be necessary (e.g., opticon, amplification, etc.)?
6. Will there need to be special arrangements for medical, psychiatric, psychological, or other consultation, etc.?
7. Will there need to be specific management techniques devised for this student?

## Sample Letter to Parents

Dear __________________________:

Your child has been tentatively approved in the __________________________ program. Before this placement can be implemented, it will be necessary to do an Individualized Education Plan for ______________________________ .

This educational plan will be developed during a meeting in which you and the professionals involved will agree on a projected program. In attendance at this meeting, the school will be represented by __________________________ (Principal), __________________________ (Teacher), and __________________________ (Psychologist). We would like both parents to attend if possible, and you should feel free to bring any person who may contribute to this meeting.

Please bring any records or notes that may be of assistance in the planning. At this meeting, you will also be asked to sign a statement of due process, which is the legal agreement for your child's placement.

Please call __________________________ and give three alternative times when you would be available for this meeting.

Very truly yours,

____________________________________

## What If's

Experience indicates that the same questions are raised over and over again by teachers. In dealing with parents, teachers have problems keeping a focus on the task at hand. Second, teachers frequently are not comfortable explaining or interpreting the law.

1. What if the parents demand/request to see the psychological assessment? Under the new confidentiality law, the parent has the right to see what is in the folder. Unless a psychologist is present to interpret the information, however, you may indicate that this is a planning session for the educational needs and offer to schedule another meeting with a psychologist present.
2. What if the parent gets off task and tries to discuss the school system, another child, etc.? Try to refocus on the assessment data without commenting on the other issues.
3. What if the parent demands more programming than you have? Outline the program that you are prepared to offer, being as reasonable as possible. If no agreement can be reached, stop the meeting. The next meeting should be scheduled with the appropriate administrators to answer that problem (or it may go to a due process hearing).
4. What if the parent does not understand the educational jargon? The presiding professional has an obligation to redefine the information.

## Most Common Questions

1. What is an IEP?

   An IEP is an individualized education plan designed specifically to meet unique needs of the Education for All Handicapped Children Act of 1975.

2. What is the least restrictive environment?

   IDEA (PL94-142) stipulates a child may not be withdrawn from his regular peers until all efforts to meet his needs through modification have proved inadequate. He may be removed only for instruction in those areas in which he cannot otherwise be maintained.

3. What is the duration of an IEP?

   All IEPs are subject to review and evaluation one year from their inception.

4. What is the length of the IEP?

   The IEP must be as long as necessary to cover the unique needs of your child. It can run from one to 30 pages.

5. What is the average time for an IEP conference?

   An IEP conference must cover the testing and the data available. Most IEP meetings last from 30 minutes to an hour.

## Administration Notes

Once the student has been approved for service, the IEP has been written, and the due process signed, consideration should be given to the following points:

1. Have arrangements been made to introduce the student to the special education teacher and room?
2. Will there be a need to change the homeroom placement because of the location of the resource room?
3. Will the regular special education teacher have time to work out mutual schedules and instructional strategies?
4. Who is responsible for a calendar of follow-up meetings?
5. Has special transportation been arranged if necessary?
6. Have arrangements been made for the supportive services that have been written in the IEP, for example, speech, language, and adaptive physical education?
7. Is audio visual equipment available that may be needed, such as a cassette player, language master, and typewriter?
8. Is there a need for other professional follow-up, such as a social worker or psychologist?
9. Has the student been notified and prepared for this change in his life?
10. Are you familiar with the regulations governing the records of special students? If not, look up the Buckley Amendment and your district policy on the confidentiality of student records. The records of special students are not only governed by law, but by compliance tied to federal funding. Do not overlook this component of placement.

## Documentation of Individual Placement Decision

After the IEP has been written and agreed upon, the administrator must present a worksheet indicating how the placement decision was made. Most school districts have a formalized procedure. The worksheet must show what placement options were considered and why. Our local district uses a form that provides three options and has developed a matrix that shows what service can be provided in any of the three options. The services to be considered include:

- Curriculum
- Related services
- Special media material
- Other learning needs
- Social/psychological needs
- Physical/medical
- Academic integration with non-exceptional students
- Negative academic integration with non-exceptional students
- Proximity to home

This worksheet is presented to the parents to confirm how the decision for special education recommendation was reached. It is presented as informational but does not require agreement or disagreement.

After the presentation of this documentation, the Notice of Recommended Assignment (NORA—the Pennsylvania due process form. See Chapter One.) is presented for signature. This gives permission to the district to remove the child from regular education for the stipulated services.

CHAPTER SIX

# Implementing the IEP

Your IEPs are done legally as IDEA (PL94-142) mandates. Now the question is what to do with them. If these IEPs are placed in the student's file and put away, they are worthless. To be effective, they must be implemented—and that means a *direct link* to daily lesson plans. Teachers who use IEPs most effectively have them on their desks and plan diagnostic teaching directly from the IEP. These teachers are one hunderd percent accountable and are able to provide helpful, verified data at any due process hearing. Ongoing planning becomes routine and is really quite simple since "the big picture" is always there.

## Sample Lesson Plan

| | John | Mary |
|---|---|---|
| **Monday** | Teach final consonants *k* and *ck*<br><br>Board words:<br>fork check<br>blank clock<br>tank stick<br><br>Can deduce rule, verbalize, ask for volunteer<br>Use follow-up worksheet, Continental Press<br><br>Continental worksheet score | Use Stern blocks<br>Have student build all combinations, 1 to 9<br>Point out step pattern<br>Student verbalize sequence<br><br>Use Stern worksheet, p. 46<br><br>Stern worksheet score |

As you can see, the above lesson plan is directly related to educational tasks on the IEP.

Teachers are encouraged to make notes directly on their lesson plans relevant to the student's performance. Thus, these notes determine if the lesson must be retaught or reviewed. In addition, teachers are encouraged to retain specific test worksheets in a folder with child's name for purposes of accountability.

This system as outlined can provide a quick check for supervisor or administrator, who should be able to trace an unmarked checklist item to the IEP and lesson plan on any given student. In addition, a supervisor should be alert to a skill that is being retaught too frequently and should be able to offer suggestions on different techniques or materials.

## Grading Policy

Idea (PL94-142) has led inevitably to some administrative problems that are detrimental to the programming of handicapped students. The concept of placing students in the least restrictive environment (LRE) has led to some integration and some innovative programming that is frequently undermined by lack of a firm, fair grading policy.

Regular teachers are troubled by "giving" a better grade to special students than they give to regular students. Special education personnel realize it is both unfair and unrealistic to evaluate handicapped students by norm-referenced standards.

Grading contracts can be established in the transition plan or graduation criteria. Student and teacher contracts could be established with timelines, extra credit bonus, quantity and quality of work for a passing or failing grade.

In effect, we have told special students that if they came into special rooms and worked hard, they would succeed. How then do we give them marginal or failing grades?

This problem takes on added significance when formal credit for graduation credits is involved. Administrators are anxious not to devaluate their diplomas and thus resist the "watering down" of criteria.

Fundamentally, these issues should be settled before problems arise. It should be recognized that regular education teachers are not being unkind, cruel, or unfeeling by maintaining academic standards. It should also be recognized that special teachers are not being unethical or unreasonable in expecting cooperative compensatory consideration for grading handicapped students.

One way of handling this is to form contracts. Let the teachers work out reasonable criteria, naming exactly what it will take to earn an A, B, or C. In this model, both the time extensions (schedules) and modifications need to be spelled out. This method is clear, but very time consuming.

Another model is one that has proven effective in cooperative school districts. In this model the student is graded by the regular education teacher for totally integrated subjects, the special education teacher for totally special subjects, and a grade arrived at jointly for subjects in which the student participates in the regular program with modifications. When the grade is established in anything but the norm-referenced way, the modifications are listed, and attached to the letter grade.

There are certainly many other possibilities and probably many other methods in operation. The main thing is that a definitive policy be established early and explained to everyone involved, so that program implementation progresses smoothly.

Some of the suggestions for program modification are as follows:

1. Preferential seating
2. Reduced assignments
3. Alternate assignments
4. Extended time lines
5. Special materials such as graph paper, felt tip markers, specially lined paper, etc.

6. Use of film strips or overhead projector to provide more/better visual material
7. Taping of content material
8. Provide peer reader/tutor
9. Test being read orally
10. Acceptance of a special project in lieu of a report
11. Calculators/Franklin Spellers
12. Multiplication matrix
13. List of commonly misspelled words
14. An assignment notebook
15. A daily schedule pasted on the inside of a notebook to be checked off
16. Multiple choice or true/false versions of test in lieu of essay completion
17. Performance contract
18. Taped (as opposed to written) reports
19. An oral examination
20. Credits for class participation

One serious and ongoing consideration for learning handicapped students in regular education classrooms is quantity versus quality. An assignment of twenty problems may well be overwhelming and never come back completed. An assignment of four problems (which might even be put on separate index cards) will be more likely to be completed. Arrangements can be made in which one card returned equals a D; two cards returned equals a C; three cards returned equals a B; and four cards returned equals an A. If the school handles the reduced assignment concept correctly, it should satisfy their progress objectives since quality minus quantity should be an index of success.

Another modification relating to reduced assignments is the written report required in many content courses. A reasonable alternative would be an outline of the main ideas and details, which is usually far easier and more reasonable for a learning disabled student.

A pictorial report using magazine or newspaper pictures with appropriate captions or explanations is another possibility. This allows the learning handicapped student to demonstrate comprehension of subject matter without regard to writing competence.

Written language output, like math, should be reduced with the emphasis on quality rather than quantity.

Some teachers might want to ask the student about assignments. Learning handicapped students are sometimes very perceptive about their own problems and can save hours of other testing.

Many teachers have found lists helpful, and the following example can be easily modified upward for secondary students with different or higher level skills.

Please check the statements that pertain to you:

1. Reading is hard for me.
2. The following textbooks are hard for me to read:
   a. Social Studies
   b. Health
   c. Science
3. The reading assignments I have to read are too long in:
   a. Social Studies

b. Health
c. Science

4. I can't spell well enough to take notes.
5. I can't read my notes.
6. When taking a test, I can't remember the right words.
7. It is hard for me to use a dictionary since I can't spell.
8. Handwriting is hard for me.
9. I like:
10. I dislike:

## The Most Critical Variable

Students would not be placed in special education if they could learn by completing one spiritmaster after another. Facilitating is grossly overrated for special students. Regardless of what supportive materials you can commandeer or how many or how few instructional materials you can negotiate, the critical difference will be made by *active direct teaching.* Research supports this statement, and common sense dictates that we employ vigorous teaching with special students. We need to:

— Direct their attention.
— State the teaching goals.
— Model the thinking process (verbalize your own thought process).
— Try multi-input, e.g., chalkboard, repetition (over-learning).
— Provide examples and non-examples.
— Provide for student input and practice.
— Have students summarize what has been learned. What was the teaching objective?
— Provide lesson closure.
— Assign independent practice. (Most LD students have poor written skills. When a teacher insists that a student "write it down," that will create the practice needed for long-term memory and provide a format that will eventually lead to written skills.)

Other models of direct teaching are commonly used and can be effective. The point is that teaching needs to be *active.* Students are usually behind academically when they enter special education, and, in fact, it is a condition of placement for some disabilities. When a teacher follows a publisher page for page, it would appear obvious that "catching up" is unlikely if not impossible. A critical concept with an academic IEP is that you teach the skills on the IEP. You find the page or unit in a textbook, and once that skill is mastered, return to the IEP for the next objective to teach. In other words, skip around the text and tear pages out of the workbook as needed to teach the skill. Your curriculum is the IEP, not the textbook. In summary, teachers are the critical difference for special education students who need to be taught vigorously. They need to exercise professional judgment routinely: When they do this, they do *make a difference.*

## Expanded Services

The expansion of services, as mandated by Public Law 101-476, October 30, 1990, has created a need for pre-graduation and post-school services plans for the transition of special students into the world of work and independent living. Many of these plans will require services beyond traditional academic teaching, and inter-agency participation will be required.

The major components are listed below.

1. Present educational levels.
   a. The results of the student's instructional evaluation
   b. The coordinated set of activities based on the student's needs, taking into account the student's preferences and interests
   c. The student's interests, abilities, and aptitudes
2. Post-school outcomes
   a. Post-secondary education
   b. Vocational training
   c. Integrated employment (including supported employment)
   d. Continuing and adult education
   e. Adult services
   f. Independent living
   g. Community participation
   h. Post-school outcomes in:
      Employment
      Post secondary education/training
      Community living
3. The student's program placement including:
   a. Student's level of intervention
   b. Location of the intervention
   c. Type of service
   d. Date placement services begin and end and anticipated duration of services
   e. Adaptations needed for success in regular education class while participating with non-exceptional students
   f. Description of programs/activities in which a student will participate with non-exceptional students
   g. Exit criteria by which it may be determined that the student is no longer in need of special education services
4. Related services and/or support services
   a. If services are an integral part of the program, and
   b. Date of beginning and duration of such services
5. Statement of inter-agency responsibilities
   a. When appropriate, define linkage/or responsibilities before the student leaves school
   b. The person or agency responsible for post-school transition
6. An indication that the IEP team has considered:
   a. Assistive technology
   b. Vocational education
   c. Extended school year programs
   d. Adaptive physical education
   e. Behavior management programs

f. Transition services (preparation for adult life)
g. Enrichment and advancement

7. IEP team participants and meeting date, signature, title, position, and affiliation of IEP team participants and date of meeting.
8. Annual goals/objectives/activities based on learning needs identified in the evaluation report
   a. Short-term learning outcomes/short-term instructional objectives/coordinated set of activities
   b. Objective criteria and/or assessment techniques for determining if learning outcomes have been achieved
   c. Dates services begin and end and their anticipated duration.

Transition Services—Section 602(a) is amended by inserting the following new paragraph:

The term "transition services" means a coordinated set of activities for a student, designed within an outcome-oriented process, which promotes movement from school to post-school activities, including post-secondary education, vocational training, integrate employment (including supported employment), continuing and adult education, adult services, independent living, or community participation. The coordinated set of activities shall be based upon the individual student's needs, taking into account the student's preferences and interests, and shall include instruction, community experiences, the development of employment and other post-school adult living objectives, and when appropriate, acquisition of daily living skills and functional vocational evaluation.

## Outcome/Post-School Requirements

The student services that are new requirements under IDEA need to be addressed at the student's 16th birthday.

These services are to be designed to coordinate activities from the school to the student's future work place (e.g., interests, needs, preferences, vocational training, etc.).

Many students may be planning to attend a local community college or university program. These students will need graduation planning to insure all appropriate high school credits have been selected for the diploma and education entrance requirements.

Students planning on attending a technical trade school or military service need to focus their high school subject selection toward that goal. Work study programs are also available in most high schools and used to plan and provide actual job training toward post-school graduation. These goals can and should be an addendum to the IEP.

The school district, parents, and the professional team should begin this dialogue before the sixteenth birthday to increase the probability of implementation of this plan.

Many states are presently writing guidelines to implement the requirements of IDEA and may not have procedures in place.

As can be seen, the job of the special education team has been greatly expanded. These IEP's need a broader objective based than the academic based IEP designed for basic skills, but the model remains the same: (1) Identify the needs with a good evaluation; (2) determine what needs to be taught in teachable units (task analysis); (3) define a hierarchical, step-by-step program with attention to pre-requisite skills; (4) define specific outcomes that can be measured; and (5) keep the focus on those identified objectives.

Examples of vocational and behavioral IEPs have been included in Appendix Three.

CHAPTER SEVEN

# Program Management

Individualized programming is hard work! It calls for complete commitment on the part of the teacher because the work is never really done. Many hours need to be spent on planning various schedules and activities so that the teacher is free to individualize. One of the persistent problems is that of managing students who are not being instructed. Even minimum grouping requires intimate knowledge of precisely what skills are indicated on the IEP.

Students enter and leave the room at various times throughout the day, and true to their handicapped stereotype, many students just do not sit still. The whole scenario is complicated by supervisors who demand active teaching and related activities.

The first few months in a resource room or special classroom can be a devastating experience for both teacher and student. The student enters the situation with no real expectations and a history of failure and acting out behavior. Teachers either enter the profession from the university where they have been buoyed up with idealism and enthusiasm or enter from a traditional teaching situation. It only takes a few days for the teacher to realize she is totally overwhelmed. Of course, the special student now becomes truly special because he/she frequently is in charge of the room. The structure of regular education has been exchanged for a permissive environment where nothing is expected and he/she can do no wrong.

The key for solving the situation is structure, structure, and more structure. A valuable way to assist teachers in providing a good program is to give them a checklist of all the things:

A. that they should be doing,

B. that they will be evaluated on by a supervisor.

The checklist which follows on the next page lists most of the variables that go into operating an individualized program successfully.

## Checklist

Educational Planning

1. Lesson plans are in evidence.
   Lesson plans are adequate.
2. Lesson(s) are geared to student need.
3. Lesson is clear and specific.
4. Academic IEPs available: dated.
5. IEPs correlated with lesson plans.

Scheduling

6. Student schedules are provided and followed.
7. Teacher is seldom interrupted by students.

Room Structure

8. A variety of activities are provided.
9. The room and activities are well organized.
10. Room is neat and uncluttered.

Management

11. Is discipline appropriate?
12. Specified management techniques used
    OC CM Modeling
13. Students are maintained on tasks consistently.

Respect for Students

14. Students are treated courteously.

Teaching Process

15. Teacher is engaged in active teaching.
    A. Gives students opportunity to verbalize
    B. Prepared
    C. Sequence instruction
    D. Questioning techniques
16. Follow-up activities are provided after instruction.
17. Independent work is relevant and appropriate.
18. Students receive feedback on academic tasks.

Learning Centers

19. Independent work is relevant and appropriate.
20. Learning centers are individualized.

## Implementing the Supervisor's Checklist

Over the years, teachers and teaching supervisors have frequently been in an adversary position. Most people want to do a good job, and certainly teachers, for the most part, are anxious to demonstrate their competency and effectiveness. What is seldom underscored is that supervisors want to do a good job and be viewed positively. The natural anxiety of being observed is frequently overshadowed by the teachers' conviction that they are not appreciated or evaluated on their real strengths. They become defensive and angry when their practices are challenged. We have found that "guessing" can be taken out of evaluation by telling teachers ahead of time precisely what will be evaluated and how. This system has eventually evolved in maintaining a checklist. No longer does a teacher have to speculate on "what are they looking for this year?" The checklist approach answers this question: "What we are looking for this year is precisely what we looked for last year. There will be no surprises."

In addition, every teacher may be assured that every item on the list will be checked off. This makes for a fair and objective observation. For example, if a teacher lacks completed or good lesson plans, the entire observation is not lost. The good teaching techniques will be evaluated and weighed. By contrast, the reverse is true; a teacher cannot ride a good reputation without performing; the halo effect will not carry on to subsequent evaluations. A dazzling teaching performance will not mask poor classroom organization. While this approach is demanding, teachers do perceive it as fair and relevant.

## Applying the Supervisor's Checklist

### Educational Planning

***Look to see if plans are in evidence and complete enough to be followed by a sub.***

Planning is an integral part of teaching. If this is true for teachers in general, it is doubly true for special education educators. It is impossible to operate an individualized program without extensive planning. It is important that plans contain the special teaching objective as well as material to be used. Page numbers should be included. Just as important as the teaching segment are the follow-up activities. Teachers need to look at follow-up activities critically and not permit publishers to determine their progress by routinely assigning the next workbook page, for it may not be the specific skill the student is working on. At this point, consideration should be given to teacher-made worksheets, center activities, manipulatives, games, audio-visual assignments, or peer tutoring as alternatives to the next workbook page.

Planning should also include what stimuli would be used and how it will be presented. It is also important to be specific—students' names in time slots in the plans so a sub can teach the right lesson to the right student. Many subs report that they must rely on students for this kind of information.

***Contingency plans are available.***

Good planners frequently solve the sub problem by making a set of contingency plans. Contingency plans are a full one-day program that is very general and includes worksheets and activities with complete directions. Contingency plans, which are applicable but not what the teacher would be doing, have several advantages for a one-day stint.

- If the teacher has the plan book at home and must be absent, alternate plans are available.
- Teachers need not worry about what will be presented for the ongoing educational program.

- It ensures the continuity of the program since the teacher moves from the last day to the next according to his/her own style.
- Since the sub has all the worksheets and activities, students are not encouraged to direct the activities with such remarks as, "No, we are on that page. She doesn't make us do it that way. She doesn't make us do it all."

### *Lesson is matched to student's needs.*

Supervisors will take a particular interest in examining a student's needs. This implies that the teacher will become familiar enough with the student through reading background information and working with the student that instruction will be planned that teaches one specific skill to one specific child in one specific way. The teacher who plans a totally verbal presentation for every student will certainly be suspect.

Psychologists frequently describe problem areas and I.Q. subscales. While not cast in stone and not always educationally relevant, this information is a beginning that teachers can explore. Next, teachers should make notes at the beginning of the year, after various kinds of presentations, as to how the student appears to learn information. Experienced teachers assimilate a great deal of information without even realizing it. New teachers need to be sensitive to these cues and signs in the student and to develop a working hypothesis about the learning style of each student. For example, one reading lesson may be strongly visual in presentation, with the chalkboard used extensively and attention paid to picture clues. A reading lesson at the same level for a different child may be highly verbal with a great deal of discussion.

Supervisors will want to see a wide variety of approaches in the plans. This will really confirm the heterogeneous make-up of the student. Resource rooms/special classrooms are not very special if instruction does not vary to meet student needs. The critical difference between a really special program and a humdrum one is the ability to provide unique instruction.

Supervisors will want to make sure the quality of the program is maintained or upgraded through a vigilant and continuous program that involves matching teaching instruction to learner needs.

### *Lesson is clear and specific.*

Skilled teaching requires lessons that are highly specific in nature. Through task analysis, large teaching objectives are reduced to small increments. This is contrary to many lessons outlined in teaching manuals that tend to embrace several objectives and levels. It is highly important that teachers zero in specifically on a teaching goal and not "wander all over the place" with their lessons. For example, a lesson on syllabication should not include lessons on vowels and digraphs at the same time. If the stimulus is a word like *envelope,* do not waste time talking about short *e* or signal *e* when trying to get the student to decode the word. Of course, the teacher should select a stimulus word within the child's vocabulary but, if, as often happens, the student doesn't know that word that day, the word should be supplied and the teaching time and focus should not be side-tracked by an impromptu lesson on vowels. (A teacher notebook is handy for this purpose.) This whole scenario can be avoided when the stimulus words and methods of presentation are clearly thought out ahead of time and written into the plans. Care should be exercised in determining how the lesson will be introduced, exactly what will be covered, and how it will be summarized. Follow-through activities should be determined and written into the plans. That is what planning is for.

*Academic IEPs are available and dated and correlated with lesson plans.*

The IEP for a special child, if used correctly, is the most important bonus to special children emanating from IDEA (PL94-142). In this legal document, plans are made for specific remediation for special problems. However, the IEP is only useful if it is used. When it is written by administrators and maintained in the central office to demonstrate legal compliance, it serves no purpose for the student. Likewise, when the teacher files the IEP in a neat little file and doesn't look at it, it serves no purpose for the student. The IEP is a working paper and the more dog-eared and worn out it looks, the more likely it is to be of value for the student. Supervisors must be sure that IEPs are used. To do this, IEPs must be checked and, indeed, IEP dates and deadlines are administrative business. However, effective supervisors will be far more interested in confirming that IEP goals are being actively pursued by daily lesson plans.

Supervisors should also check groupings in IEPs. Group instruction is not contrary to individualized teaching provided that each student in the group needs that skill, is at the instructional level for that skill, and has a learning need compatible to the instruction being planned. However, these are tough conditions to meet, and in a room with special students, not only are they difficult but the charting to achieve grouping among highly diverse students is time consuming. Supervisors will want to make sure that any grouping done in a resource room or special classroom meets all of the above conditions and is not done to suit students' schedules or teachers' convenience. One good rule of thumb is that unless it is in the IEP, participation in a group is inappropriate.

Teachers need to be aware that supervisors will be monitoring students' progress and thus checking the correlation between lesson plans and IEPs as a responsible part of their routine duties.

## Students' Schedules

In our experience, scheduling students is very often the cornerstone on which the success or failure of the room hinges. Given the proposition that special students frequently lack initiative, motivation, and independent skills, the teacher cannot rely on their staying productively employed. As one student is taught, there are other students who must be planned for appropriately. It is unrealistic to expect these students to maintain on-task behavior without specific directions. Making individual student schedules has provided a way of structuring the entire day in advance. Let's suppose a teacher works in 15 minute increments with individual students. The first task is to block out the day in 15 minute increments for each child. After filling in any special class such as art, gym, or music, the teacher pencils in the specific 15 minute block that she will be involved in direct teaching of that student according to her lesson plans. This, of course, may involve several teaching blocks a day. The remaining blocks need to be filled in with a variety of purposeful activities. This is highly important for several reasons.

- The student knows where he/she will be every minute of the day.
- The student knows exactly what he/she is to do every minute of the day.
- Equipment like Language Masters, tape recorders, typewriters, and filmstrips can only be used by one person at a time and requires scheduling.
- If you are fortunate enough to have an aide, her time also needs to be allocated.
- This persistent referencing and monitoring of time assists students to internalize the passing of time and helps them to develop some sense of time segments.

Schedules can be the crux of structure in a special room *only* if they are used. This requires that students be taught a scheduling system and refer to it constantly. In the beginning of the year, the questions should always be, "What are you scheduled to do now?" "Are you on this schedule?" "Are you scheduled to be here?" This constant referencing reinforces the principle that the schedule tells them what to do during the day. This frees the teacher to teach without constantly placing students in activities. Several sample schedules are provided in Appendix 4.

It should be noted that supervisors can always tell when the teacher has done a "show and tell." When teachers actually paste schedules on the students' desks for the supervisor's benefit, it only takes a few minutes to recognize the structure is not working for the teacher and has, in fact, been an exercise in additional paper work. When scheduling is effective, it reflects a persistent effort on the part of the teacher early in the year and frequently appears as if the room runs itself. On the other hand, the scheduling imposes restrictions on the teacher as well as the student. Lessons must be timed and on time. Many teachers use a timer set for 15 minute intervals. When the timer rings, it signals a change of activities for everyone, and the teacher must have their lessons timed to coincide with students' schedules.

*Some of the scheduled activities include physical movement.*

Teachers are not going to prevent students from getting restless and moving around. Good scheduling can reduce this to a minimum by building appropriate movement into the schedule. Students can move from their desk to a center and 15 minutes later move to still another center. Paper and pencil tasks can be alternated with audiovisual assignments, and some activities can be planned that actually utilize physical movement, such as pacing off arithmetic problems. Providing an appropriate outlet for students' restlessness is good planning since it is bound to occur anyhow.

*Teacher is seldom interrupted by students.*

One of the positive rewards for teachers who are willing to invest a great deal of time in scheduling is the prospect of being free to teach. There can be very little incentive to this additional activity if you are constantly interrupted. All teachers need to be sensitive to students' needs. Firm guidelines must be set for students by establishing and demanding exact teaching time. It is almost axiomatic that teachers who tolerate interruptions have more and more interruptions. After seeing that students' work is on the appropriate level, teachers need to refuse all interruptions from students except the youngster they are directly instructing. Demands for exact attention can be met in several ways:

— Questions can be referred to the aide.
— Questions can be referred to a designated peer.
— Every two or three hours, a consolidation block can be set aside. During that period, the teacher is available.
— When the bell rings between periods, the teacher may answer questions briefly.
— The teacher issues two or three question passes to each student a day. When these passes are used up, there are no more questions available until the next day.
— Students may have an oaktag card with the word "HELP" written on it. This card is displayed when the student wants assistance. The student works on some other task until the teacher responds to the "HELP" flag.

Clever teachers always find ways to deal with problems of interruption, and there are certainly many other techniques available. The point is that every teacher must develop some technique or system to control interruptions or there will never be time to teach. Good supervisors are not interested in knowing how the objective is achieved but will comment negatively if the teacher is continuously interrupted during instruction.

## Room Structure

One important aspect of individual instruction is the need for a full variety of activities. This is especially true of special students who have a short attention span. It is highly important that variety includes activities geared toward visual and tactile. If you believe that a special youngster has a limited attention span, changing the mode of stimuli makes common sense. Some suggestions might include: Language Master, cassette player, viewmaster, record player, pocket games, calculator, Systems 80, TV games, and physical games aimed at academic remediation (e.g., bean bags, dice, egg cartons, and pocket charts with word combinations). The list is only limited by the extent of the teacher's imagination. Good practice would suggest that youngsters be scheduled for a highly verbal activity followed by a visual activity, and so forth.

One of the basic concepts of altering the activities by a schedule is tied to reality inasmuch as students will only stay on a task so long, and then will move on. By changing the activity and tying it to a schedule, the teacher gains control of the situation. Teachers can have students doing activities that are needed and productive by scheduling the movement to capture what students do anyhow.

If the room is to have maximum structure, it must be well organized with activities and supplies accessible to students. This means that items like scissors, crayons, and paper should be placed where students can get them when needed. Assigned work should be kept in individual folders on the students' desks. It is also preferable that the student have a box or file for completed work. Many teachers have a completed work box on their desk. This results in a steady stream of students marching to the teacher's desk, which is distracting and unnecessary.

Many teachers chart activities near a learning center so students can maintain their own progress. This reinforces completion and sets up a pattern of evaluation against past performance instead of against another student. The physical arrangement of the room must be consistent with the room size and contain physical attributes of the room as well as teaching style of the teacher. In general, there are a few characteristics to look for:

- The teacher has a teaching table which is where teaching takes place in this room.
- All teaching should be done at the teaching table and other activities like seatwork or visiting are prohibited.
- The teaching table should be directly in front of the chalkboard and other teaching supplies such as manuals should be near by.
- Student desks or stations should be away from the teaching table in space and face outward. Otherwise, students may "join in" every lesson.
- Audio-visual stations and other centers should be distanced across from the teacher so she can monitor across the room but not be interrupted by the sound.
- If students are distractible, they can frequently be faced into a wall or filing cabinet to reduce visual distractions.
- A grouping of four or six desks or a small table should be provided for students to work together when assigned
- The aide should be stationed as far from the teacher as possible. Experience shows that frequently the aide's position results in teacher and aide competing for the same space.
- Certain classroom rules need to operate. Rules relating to sharpening pencils, going into the bathroom, or going after supplies need to be enforced to reduce constant motion.

- As much as possible, work checking or answer centers need to be provided so students can check their work.
- A "HELP" section where multiplication answer charts, calculator, or model problems are kept as a resource serves to reduce information-seeking questions. This promotes independence since it sends students to the kind of sources teachers want them to use. Obviously, a center with answers needs monitoring by the teacher to be used appropriately.
- An activity table with puzzles, games, or other electives needs to be provided so students who finish work quickly have an automatic assignment that is rewarding while keeping them occupied. This is an excellent place for bonus activities.

All classrooms reflect a certain style of the teacher, building, and grade level. Some teachers are very neat while others operate best in more casual surroundings. However, special education teachers have a special duty to provide good modeling for their students. One example that comes to mind is the LD child who cannot get organized and collected for instruction. When the room is not neat and organized, this student has no way to pull himself/herself together and collect needed material to work. Therefore, while neatness is not a prerequisite of teaching, a neat and uncluttered room for a special student is desired since it helps organize the world for him/her. In addition, maintaining a neat, uncluttered room forces prepared organization on the teacher, and this is reflected in a more organized program for the student.

## Management

The most critical aspect of teaching special students is frequently student management. The best teacher in the world cannot teach if the students are disruptive. In regular education, teachers work with students as a group and then assign work so that they may circulate and maintain discipline. The task for the special education teacher is much more involved and difficult. While the teacher works with one or two students, all other students must be occupied. Good programming demands that the student be occupied with meaningful work, not busy work. The scope of the problem becomes apparent when one realizes that in an individual program, each student may only be involved with the teacher once or twice for fifteen minute periods during a day. The rest of the time, the student must be maintained in a productive, orderly fashion. Discipline in this situation can very quickly get out of control. Based on these difficulties, it is not surprising that many teachers have discipline problems. The question of discipline can be addressed in two ways. Discipline can be negative or positive. The research on negative discipline supports the fact that it *usually* works. The problem is that it does not usually make good students, and, therefore, most special educators are opposed to negative discipline. Discipline with positive reinforcement is a much better tool since it is ultimately aimed at giving students a chance to internalize appropriate behavior and to be intrinsically motivated.

Supervisors will look carefully at whatever method is used in the room and assess whether it is appropriate for the particular child or specific offense. Consistency is probably the hallmark of good discipline, and the beginning teacher should be aware that unless discipline is applied, there will surely be little or no discipline in the room regardless of the system.

Supervisors will make note of discipline problems. Good supervisors will observe various management systems in operation and be prepared to offer assistance for problem cases.

- One of the more common systems is operant conditioning. This is most commonly what people mean when they say behavior mod. Based on Skinner's S-R model, operant conditioning holds that whatever behavior is reinforced will be most likely to reoccur. At the teaching level, teachers are usually admonished to "catch them being good." They are to reinforce the behavior that they want whenever they find it occurring. Theory suggests that if the teacher continues to reinforce it either with chips, points, or praise every time it occurs, it will soon be occurring with great regularity. At this point, the reinforcement is reduced or put on a schedule.

One important aspect of this is to find what is reinforcing to the child. Good students who are intrinsically motivated work for grades. With special students, this usually is impossible because there are no good grades and the student is not intrinsically motivated.

The cheapest reinforcement for a special student is a smile or praise, but many times this simply doesn't work. Many reinforcers have been devised over the last twenty years with the special education student. Some of the more commonly used reinforcers are free time, special activities, stars, pizza parties, extra gym period, teacher attention, and, of course, more primary rewards like Cracker Jacks prizes and food. The goal is always to move the student upward toward a cheaper (smile) reinforcement and ultimately onto intrinsic motivation. A given teacher may be at a different point with different students in the room. Supervisors will note that some students get stars, other praise, and some may even get physical contact (pats). Entire books have been written on various methods of reinforcement.

— Contingency management is another technique that will be noted by astute supervisors. Contingency management is more commonly known as contracting, which, in its simplest form, may be a verbal agreement such as "When you finish your seatwork, you may play a game." It is also common to see written contracts with special education students. These may range from daily to weekly and may be two or three lines, or highly involved with parents and principals signing off. One nice aspect of contingency contracting is its versatility since it can be used for behavior, academics, or both.

— Modeling is another management technique that is instantly apparent and highly effective. Teachers who use this tell students by example the specific behavior that they like or expect by their positive comments to, or about, another student. (For example, "I like the way Joe is looking at me. That tells us that he is ready to listen." or "Mary, can you show Kelly how your paper is headed? That is exactly how I want it.")

Modeling is perhaps more effective with younger students who are still eager to gain teacher approval and should be used cautiously with students above the primary level since it may set an older student up as a scapegoat or may not be reinforcing to students seeking peer approval.

Many other management techniques are used, and some teachers appear to manage students almost effortlessly by the force of their personality. In any event, supervisors will make note of the management system used, if basic room rules are posted, the amount of positive reinforcement used, and, most important, the level of control evident in the room.

Good classroom management by the teacher will ultimately be reflected in good on-task behavior by the students. Common sense dictates that students who work consistently will achieve consistently. Most supervisors will be very quick to note if the on-task behavior of the students is not good. Students who are not working are usually not just sitting but are obviously engaged in non-productive behavior like talking, moving around, or playing with objects. Keeping students on-task requires considerable teacher skill in providing the correct amount of appropriate work and constant monitoring of the classroom even when the teacher is working on direct instruction with other students.

## Respect for Students

A critical aspect of the operation of any classroom is the teacher's attitude toward the students. With special education students this is doubly so since they frequently have low self-concepts and poor interpersonal relations. Many special students are exasperating and difficult to like. Added to this is a threat to the teacher's self-esteem since the special student seldom reinforces the teacher by learning and thus poses a professional failure.

Teachers must differentiate between the actor and the act. You may not like Johnny's running around the classroom, but Johnny must be told that it is the running, not him, that upsets you. Students must be assured that academic mistakes or failure to learn do not make them bad or worthless.

Supervisors will be quick to note if a teacher is sarcastic or uses disparaging terms. They might also want to note examples of discourtesy. Many teachers fail to extend common courtesy to children and treat them differently than they treat adults. Where are children to learn consideration and manners if not in school? It is easy to embarrass or belittle a student; it takes professional skill to correct and reteach without offending.

Respect and consideration should not be confused with babying or patronizing. Students should not be called "honey" or other "pet" names. Teachers should neither encourage nor accept familiarity from a student.

It should be noted that young teachers frequently try to become too friendly with adolescents. This is a mistake since it invites familiarity and is occasionally misinterpreted by special education adolescents who read it as a "come on." The role of the teacher should be a professional one.

## Teaching Process

### *Active Teaching*

While supervisors (and others) may observe and comment on other issues, *teaching* is the major focus in any teacher evaluation. Active teaching has several innate characteristics regardless of teaching style.

- Active teaching involves an interaction between student and teacher. The student must be an active participant in the process or it is a performance, not teaching.
- The teacher must have a goal that is specifically defined. If the teacher doesn't know where the lesson is headed, how can she get there? Next, active teaching requires preparation. Preparation includes knowing how the lesson is to be presented. Will the board be used or will visual aids be needed? What example will be used or what analogies? How are students to be involved—what are they expected to say or do? How will this lesson be linked to previous learning to facilitate retention and application?
- In addition, teaching has a definite sequence. The most commonly used method that is usually used for skill teaching is: (a) Introduction (tell them what they're going to

learn); (b) Content (present the lesson, give many examples and non-examples, involve the students, and so forth); and (c) Summarize (either get or give a statement of what has been learned).

Other types of lessons, such as problem solving, have a different sequence. Good supervision will identify the model of presentation and detect inferior techniques quickly. This will certainly be a prime target for teacher improvement.

— Another technique area of scrutiny will be the questioning techniques and level of student involvement in any given presentation. Good teaching methodology will "make up" for a lot of shortcomings, but no combination of strengths will compensate for lack of real teaching competence.

### *Instructional Follow-Up*

An important component of teaching revolves around practice and application. Once a lesson is taught, follow-up activities give students a chance to practice the skill and integrate it into their repertoire. Workbook pages and spiritmasters are commonly used for this purpose. The closer the activity follows the lesson (in time), the better. In addition, the assignment should "match" the lesson. If a prepared sheet is not appropriate, good teachers make worksheets or tailor assignments to fit the lesson they plan to teach.

### *Independent Work*

All teachers are guilty of occasionally giving "busy work." Professional integrity demands that this be held to a minimum. With special students, this becomes important since:

— They are already behind and can't waste time doing useless tasks.

— They are already "turned-off" with repeated tasks that lack relevance.

— When they can't do the assignment, they get frustrated and become behavior problems.

— There are usually problems of generalizing a skill to begin with, and when work is not relevant, it complicates the integration of learning, which may already be a problem.

— It simply isn't fair to the student.

### *Student Feedback*

Teachers grow weary with paperwork, and, of course, correcting assignments and giving corrective feedback is paperwork. However, the sooner corrective feedback is made, the more effective it will be for the learner.

Many supervisors automatically check a workbook selected at random or a folder of completed work. When student work is uncorrected, the supervisor is alerted, for subsequent work will usually deteriorate. This will happen first because of misinformation (the student thinks he's right when he's not), and, secondly, because lack of reinforcement will reduce student effort.

## Learning Centers

Learning centers have become mandated in our resource rooms and special classrooms. Several reasons support this requirement.

- Learning centers should have high motivation value for students since they are colorful and designed to add variety to ordinary tasks.
- They provide legitimate movement since a student "goes" to the center and leaves the center for another area when he is through. The need for providing legitimate movement cannot be overemphasized with special students. If you don't provide some movement, many special students spend time in endless trips to the pencil sharpener, restroom, or book shelf, and so forth, or, even worse, aimless wandering.
- Learning centers provide a practical way for teachers to utilize audio-visual equipment individually and to modify assignments to meet individual needs. This includes cassette players, Language Master, film previews, typewriter, overhead projector, computers, and games.
- Learning centers provide a practical way for teachers to use a wide variety of manipulatives on an individually assigned schedule based on the need of the student.
- Learning centers provide the teacher with a method of assigning practice and drill without an endless stream of dreary spiritmasters, which are all the same for all students (and therefore not appropriate for all students). It also breaks the monotony of pencil-paper work throughout the day.
- Learning centers also provide the teacher with a convenient vehicle to arrange some peer tutoring or other student-student pairing that might be highly desirable for either academic or social objectives.
- Learning centers are easily multi-leveled and thus particularly modifiable for an individualized program.

For all the reasons listed above, learning centers should be individualized. Not all students should be assigned to a center, and the assignment to a center should be predicated on the student's need for practice and readiness to benefit from the work done there.

In summary, when evaluating the teacher of an individualized program, the following points are covered:

Under Educational Planning

1. Look to see if plans are in evidence and complete enough to be followed by a sub.
2. Note if level of instruction is well sequenced and appropriate for student. Not too high, not too low.
3. Check if objective to be taught is clear and specifically stated. (For example, what is the teacher teaching and what will be used as stimuli, and so forth?)
4. Are plans directly correlated with IEP? (child specific)
5. Are IEPs working papers? Is teacher using them to plan, and are they currently dated?

Under Scheduling

6. Do students have schedules, and are the schedules appropriate for each level? (For example, clocks for primary students; checklist type or student constructed for older students)
7. Notice teacher interruptions. Are there an excessive number? What is the pattern of interruption? Is it mostly one student whose assignment is not clear or do all students interrupt?

Under Structure

8. Are there sufficient activities available in the room to provide interesting motivational independent work? Are students expected to do continuous pencil-paper tasks? Is the space limited or well utilized?
9. Does the teacher provide well organized modeling for students?
10. Is the room uncluttered and neat? (Check excessive centers, crowding, poor arrangement of desks, and so forth.)

Under Management

11. Is the room well managed or is there a discipline problem? If there is a discipline problem, how is it handled? For example, does the teacher argue with the students? (power struggle) Does the teacher ignore inappropriate behavior?
12. Check the methods of student management in use during the observation.
13. Are students consistently maintained on task? What does the teacher do if they are not on task?

Under Respect for Students

14. Is the teacher courteous to the pupils or is there sarcasm? Does teacher raise her voice? Does the teacher maintain a distance between the students? (For example, always behind a desk.)

Under Teaching Process

15. Is teacher actively engaged in teaching or supervising spiritmasters?
    A. Who does most of the talking? What is the proportion of student verbalization? (Is it less than 50%?)
    B. Is the teacher using a manual? Are lessons presented on a chalkboard? Are manipulatives used with the introduction? Does the teacher stick with a single style presentation or is there variety geared to the students' individual needs? Is the teacher sensitive to the input modality? (For example, visual, auditory, etc.)
    C. When teaching a lesson, does the teacher introduce the lesson, then cover the material with a high level of student interaction, followed by a summary of the lesson?
    D. Does the teacher consistently pose questions that can be answered with one word, or is the student challenged with open-end higher level questioning?
16. Is there a follow-up assignment to the center or in the form of seat work or drill or is homework assigned? Are instructions clear?
17. Is independent seatwork conducted at the center or in the seat? Is it at the appropriate level? Is it interesting? Are the spiritmasters clear? Is there audio-visual equipment in use?
18. Are the students' papers checked and feedback provided? Is the checking system systematic and done positively? (For example, number right instead of number wrong, etc.) Note who does the checking, the teacher or the aide.

Under Centers

19. Are the centers multi-leveled and assigned to achieve a teaching objective? Do they provide a variety of input and output options for students rather than a series of repetitive pencil-paper tasks?
20. Do the students assigned to a center need the practice or is this assigned busy work?

While all of these points are considered important, they are not equivalent. Teachers who get "yes" on questions 15 through 18 are considered *good* teachers and the thrust of supervision is to:

- Help these teachers develop competencies in any other area that was "no" or marginal.
- Reinforce these teachers through recognition, special assignments, and any available remunerative activities such as extra days during the summer or reference for private tutoring.
- Watch these teachers for potential leadership, professional growth, and eventual promotion.

When teachers have problems with questions 15 through 18, the thrust of supervision is both urgent and direct and should:

- Provide immediate assistance either in person or with a peer teacher.
- Send this teacher to spend a day with a model peer teacher.
- Provide a list of suggestions with a definite deadline, and a series of en-route check points.
- Be prepared to withhold official approvals (for example, tenure, yearly ratings).

With any other suggestions on the supervisor's checklist, negative or marginal responses result in a written list of suggestions, a tentative plan for improvement, and the offer of technical assistance upon request.

In our experience, teachers who have the supervisor's checklist in advance not only get "yes" on every measure but demonstrate a consistently high level of expertise on every measure.

## Administrative Roles

In our administration model, the supervisor functions as outlined in this chapter. The main duties revolve around teacher development and student programming. In our system the building principals are more involved with plant operations and the administration of regular education. Traditionally, they have had little to do with special education. Since the advent of IDEA (PL94-142) and subsequent mainstreaming, there has been increasing principal involvement with special students. This is particularly true in chairing IEP meetings and attending parent conferencing. Different administrative units may have a different flow chart, and many of the duties described in this chapter may currently be filled by building principals.

It seems obvious that one or two areas specifically require a supervisor (or other) who is knowledgeable in the theory of special education. The two main areas that come to mind are evaluating special education teacher performances and programming for special needs. Whether this function is carried out by the principal or supervisor, it certainly needs someone familiar with the field.

CHAPTER EIGHT

# Tips for Parents

An important new member of the educational team as defined by federal legislation IDEA (PL94-142) is the parent. Prior to creation of this law, parents were involved to the degree that an individual district chose to invite them. At best they were tolerated, and very often they were excluded from the most important aspect of the planning because they were "not professionals." IDEA has mandated that parents be consulted, involved, and included. These privileges also bring obligations. For most parents, the role of confidant/consultant is a new one, and frequently they get ambiguous, unclear messages. Professionals are not always comfortable sharing, explaining, or discussing sensitive information, and do not always communicate well. In the past, professionals have been free to discuss children using jargon, acronyms, and job-specific shorthand. Now, once parents become key members of the team, professionals are compelled to marshal their ideas (1) in plain language, (2) using defined terms, and (3) monitoring their choice of words and expressions. As a result, professionals have become wary. On the positive side, most professionals have become better record-keepers and are initiating better methods of documenting diagnostic and implementation data. On the other hand, many professionals have become "too careful" and are refusing to "put anything in writing." This is unfortunate since the value of the professionals is in interpretation and impressions, and not the actual data.

With all these changes, parents get mixed messages about their responsibilities and send back unclear answers. On the one hand, they are not always given the professional information on which to base sensible decisions; therefore, they may come into meetings with inaccurate ideas, unsatisfactory past experiences, demands, accusations, irrelevant and unrealistic expectations.

Parents can make professionals more comfortable and informative by being positive, open, and realistic. This is not always easy. The main point is to come into the meetings as a *parent.* There is no point to try to "out-profession" the professionals. Parents are not expected to be "educational experts," nor need the rest of the team be reminded of parents' legal rights. They already know them! Parents are on the team because they have highly important information that only they can supply. They should be prepared to take their rightful place on the team and contribute what they uniquely can—parental observations and input. To do this more effectively, a list of do's and don'ts has been compiled. This list is not exhaustive, but does address itself to the more common needs and pitfalls.

## Do's for Parents

1. Ask for evaluations (diagnostic/educational) if you feel that it is needed. It is your legal right, as well as responsibility, toward your child. While most referrals for testing come from teachers, parents who know their child are in a position to anticipate problems and suggest evaluative testing before the child fails and fails and fails.
2. Seek the advice of local professionals such as school administrators, psychologists, and teachers. They, too, want your child to succeed.
3. Be cooperative. Your child will benefit if you exhibit a friendly, open attitude.
4. Make yourself available for meetings. The law mandates that you be included, and professionals are cautiously willing to comply, but you have to go "half way" by being willing to attend at reasonable times. Parents who refuse to "disturb" their own schedules, and require evening and weekend meetings unnecessarily get planning off to a bad start.
5. Ask for definitions. School personnel want you to understand and will be willing to explain. You are not expected to "know it all," but they will not know what you don't know until you ask.
6. Know your child as a parent. Make notes about behaviors and schedules. You will be expected to know about:
   (a) food likes and dislikes
   (b) allergies
   (c) sleep habits: regular/irregular, amounts, etc.
   (d) TV habits: how much, what kind of programs, etc.
   (e) peer interaction: who, how long, how well, etc.
   (f) family interaction: mother, father, sister(s), brother(s), grandparents
   (g) competencies: go to the store, handle money, make bed, handle tools, dismantle a bike, do dishes, run errands, feed pet(s), etc.
   (h) communication: phone messages, phone conversations, making needs/wants known, knows family facts
   (i) emotional balance: sensitive/insensitive, tantrums, aggressive, shy, bully, cry, fight, whine, coax, listen, etc.
   (j) interests: active/inactive,fine/gross motor, constant/ever-changing
   (k) play: group/independent, destructive/constructive, organized/disorganized
   (l) discipline: how, by whom, when, how often, consistency
7. Be as positive and optimistic about your child as possible. Try to see and define him/her as a child with problems, not a "problem child."
8. Be honest and truthful. Shielding behavior and distorting information serves your child poorly. If your perception of your child is totally different from all others, you need to think about your stance. Of course, some variance for different circumstances is expected.

## Don'ts for Parents

1. Don't try to be teacher. Give professionals credit for knowing their job and for having your child's best interest at heart. Insisting that methods or materials you have heard about be used violates teacher integrity by implying she needs to be told what or how to teach.

2. Don't "bad-mouth" previous teachers or administrators. It is easy to understand how frustrated parents can become, but team meetings designed to help your child are neither the time nor the place for gripes and recriminations. It is also counterproductive.
3. Don't try to "pick-up" and/or use jargon and professional know-how during the meetings. The old adage "a little knowledge is a dangerous thing" is heard more and more these days. It usually refers to an anxious but aggressive parent who uses phrases and assesses opinions inappropriately or erroneously. If you are a professional, fine. You can "talk shop." If you are not, resist the temptation. You will be more highly regarded as a team member if you retain integrity.
4. Don't be defensive. Professionals are not assembled to judge you nor your child. You are involved because your child has a learning problem, not because you or the child are at fault.
5. Don't expect miracles. There are no "quick fixes." Many children will have persistent, life-long problems. The goals of educators are to develop the child to full potential, not to "change" or "cure" that potential. You need to be realistic and patient as well as constantly supportive. No teacher can succeed with your child if you are negative or hostile.
6. Don't dwell on mistakes. Some will be made along the way, but these should serve as learning experiences by all, not weapons of retaliation, or vindication of superior posture.
7. Don't be afraid to approach a teacher about legitimate concerns. If you do not get satisfaction, it is appropriate to go above the teacher to the supervisor or the principal, but give the teacher a chance to explain the areas of concern.
8. Don't be unreasonable about time.
   (a) Demanding that the time allotted for a meeting extend unreasonably detracts from the time the teacher can spend teaching.
   (b) Professionals do have a home life and other commitments. Be considerate about when and how much time you demand.
9. Don't be afraid or be reluctant to let others know when a good job is being done. Educators also need reinforcement.

# Appendices

APPENDIX ONE

# Math Checklist
# Reading Checklist

## Card 1

Using this picture, ask questions that will gain the information you need. For example, which clown is big? If this clown is big what is this clown?

Point to the balloon with the longest string.
Point to the clown with two balloons.
Which clown is on the left?
Point to the clown on the right.
Where is the dog?

# Math Checklist

I. ______________ will prove competent on directionality and body-image concepts.

Using Card. No. 1, ascertain if the student has the following list of concepts. As a teacher, you may choose the order of presentation, remembering that children should have colors initially and that the various terms are not only math relevant but language concepts as well. Coloring tends to be messy; therefore, it should be completed last.

1. Recognizes color (red, blue, yellow, green).
2. Recognizes structional attitudes (big/little, tall/short, long/short).
3. Identifies 1, 2.
4. Recognizes positional words (bottom/top, over/under, between, above/below, before/ after).
5. Quantity counting skills 1-10; 1-100.
6. Recognizes left to right (generalize to paper).

II. ______________ will prove competent on counting of groups and terminology.

Using a group of any common item in the classroom, have the student identify various sets of 1-12. Some suggestions might be paper clips, pieces of chalk, marbles, or any real objects.

1. Counts items in a group 1-12.
2. Can identify or use arithmetic terminology (more than/less than, largest/smallest, most/least).

III. ______________ will prove competent on number sequencing skills.

Teacher can prepare index cards, write out stimulus on a piece of paper or use a chalkboard to get the following information.

1. Fills in missing numbers in a straight number sequence both forward and backward (e.g., 1 2 __ 4 __ 6 7 8; 20 19 __ 17; etc.).
2. Sequence numbers from smallest to largest when given a group of numbers. (e.g., 7, 4, 14).
3. Recognizes and completes number patterns (forward even, backward even, forward odd, backward odd).
4. Copies and organizes number problems (forms numbers correctly, lines digits correctly, positions signs correctly, spaces decimals and dollar signs).

5. Counts aloud to teacher (1-20, backwards 20-1, by 2's, 5's, and 10's).
6. Calls printed numerals (e.g., 1-digit, 2-digit, 3-digit numbers).

IV. ______________ will prove competent on the following arithmetic processes.

Provide the student with a worksheet containing samples of a variety of math problems. Check mastery with additional problems if not exactly sure where student is encountering difficulty. For example, does he miss a problem because he lacks math facts, or does he work the problem from left to right? Notice whether he is attending to signs and if proper alignment would improve his performance. Some key concepts to check are: doubles (5 + 5, 9+ 9), adding 0 (8 + 0, 6 + 0) addition of ten to any number (6 + 10, 18 + 10).

1. Recognizes and names fractions
2. Creates fractions
3. Processes and manipulates fractions
4. Processes and manipulation (addition of like fractions, subtractions of like fractions, recognize improper fractions, recognize mixed fractions, recognize reduced fractions, determines greater than/less than using fractional parts)

V. ______________ will prove competent on the following symbol skills.

1. Recognizes and uses math signs (e.g., +, -, etc.)
   Given signs, names the process
   - plus sign
   - minus sign
   - multiplication sign
   - division sign
   - equal sign
   - greater than sign
   - less than sign
   - dollar sign
   - cent sign

VI. ______________ will prove competent on the following structural skills.

1. Recognizes and uses place value (e.g., one, tens, hundreds, etc.)
   Place value: reads and writes place value
   - one's place
   - ten's place
   - hundred's place
   - thousand's place
   - tens of thousand's place
   - hundreds of thousand's place
   - million's place
   - expanded notation
2. Rounded numbers (e.g., tens, hundreds, etc.)
3. Averages numbers (e.g., single, multiple digit)
4. Reads, constructs, and interprets graphs
   Graphs: Answers questions from a graph and constructs a graph from information
   - locate day (horizontal point)
   - locate degree (vertical point)
   - locate highest point

locate lowest point
construct horizontal information
construct vertical information
place points within matrix

VII. _______________ will improve accuracy on word-problem skills.

1. Identifies necessary process to solve one- and two-step problems.
2. Does necessary computations to solve one- and two-step problems.

VIII. _______________ will prove competent on the following measurement skills.

1. Tells and converts clock time
   - o'clock
   - quarter hour
   - half hour
   - minutes
2. Knows and uses calendar time
3. Identifies, converts and uses money
   - names penny
   - names nickel
   - names dime
   - names quarter
   - names half-dollar
   - selects coins by value
   - show amount of 76 cents
   - show amount of 56 cents
   - show amount of 33 cents
   - show amount of 15 cents
   - show amount of 27 cents
   - make change (27 cents out of 50 cents)
4. Identifies, converts, and uses linear measures
   - knows terms: inch, foot, yard
   - knows abbreviations: in., ft., yd.
   - knows signs: ' and "
   - knows how to measure
   - conversions
   - designates length with ruler
   - knows:
     - 12 inches = foot
     - 36 inches = yard
     - 3 feet = yard
     - 25 inches = 2 feet, 1 inch
     - 30 inches = 2½ feet
     - 60 inches = 5 feet
     - 8 feet = 2 yards, 2 feet
     - 3 yards = 9 feet
5. Identifies, converts, and uses weight measures
   - knows terms: ounces, pounds
   - knows abbreviations: oz., lb.
   - knows:
     - 16 oz. = 1 lb.
     - 8 oz. = ½ lb.
     - 20 oz. = 1 lb., 4 oz.
     - 1 lb., 8 oz. = 24 oz.
     - 2½ lbs., = 40 oz.

less than 1 lb.
more than 5 lbs.
more than 300 lbs.

6. Identifies, converts, and uses liquid measures
   knows terms: pint, quart, gallon
   knows abbreviations: pt., qt., gal.
   knows:
   2 cups = 1 pint
   2 pints = 1 quart
   5 pts. = 1 qt., 1 pt.
   8 pts. = 4 qts.
   4 qts. = 1 gallon
   9 qts. = 2 gal., 1 qt.
   12 qts. = 3 gals.
7. Reads and uses temperatures

IX. ________________ will prove competent in the following geometry skills.

1. Recognizes and names shapes
   circle square triangle rectangle
2. Recognizes and uses geometric terminology (e.g., point, line, segment, etc.)
   point
   line
   line segment
   parallel lines
   perpendicular lines
   ray
   right angle
   closed curve
   open curve
3. Recognizes and uses angles (using protractor, student measures)
4. Computes (e.g., area, diameter, etc.)

# Reading Checklist

I. ______________ will prove competent in the following phonic analysis skills:

1. Initial consonants:
   A. Identifies initial sound from spoken word
   B. Produces word given initial letter name

| | | A | B | | | A | B | | | A | B |
|---|---|---|---|---|---|---|---|---|---|---|---|
| (budge) | b | ___ | ___ | (leash) | l | ___ | ___ | (tab) | t | ___ | ___ |
| (jilt) | j | ___ | ___ | (seep) | s | ___ | ___ | (fad) | f, ph | ___ | ___ |
| (rye) | r | ___ | ___ | (zing) | z | ___ | ___ | (nudge) | n | ___ | ___ |
| (yen) | y | ___ | ___ | (dude) | d | ___ | ___ | (valve) | v | ___ | ___ |
| (kale) | c, k | ___ | ___ | (mope) | m | ___ | ___ | (gird) | g | ___ | ___ |
| (poach) | p | ___ | ___ | (wince) | w | ___ | ___ | (hub) | h | ___ | ___ |
| (quick) | q | ___ | ___ | (x-ray) | x | ___ | ___ | | | | |

2. Final consonants:
   A. Identifies initial sound from spoken word
   B. Produces word given initial letter name

| | | A | B | | | A | B | | | A | B |
|---|---|---|---|---|---|---|---|---|---|---|---|
| (grab) | b | ___ | ___ | (hall) | l | ___ | ___ | (love) | v | ___ | ___ |
| (midge) | j, dge, ge | ___ | ___ | (mess) | s | ___ | ___ | (flag) | g | ___ | ___ |
| (wheat) | t | ___ | ___ | (buzz) | z | ___ | ___ | (trap) | p | ___ | ___ |
| (waif) | f | ___ | ___ | (road) | d | ___ | ___ | (baby/cry) | y (e, i) | ___ | ___ |
| (clear) | r | ___ | ___ | (worm) | m | ___ | ___ | (pox) | x | ___ | ___ |
| (lac) | c, ck, k | ___ | ___ | (bran) | n | ___ | ___ | | | | |

3. Middle consonants:
   A. Identifies initial sound from spoken word
   B. Produces word given initial letter name

| | | A | B | | | A | B | | | A | B |
|---|---|---|---|---|---|---|---|---|---|---|---|
| (rabbit) | b | ___ | ___ | (bison) | s | ___ | ___ | (banner) | n | ___ | ___ |
| (major) | j | ___ | ___ | (buzzer) | z | ___ | ___ | (seven) | v | ___ | ___ |
| (carrot) | r | ___ | ___ | (today) | d | ___ | ___ | (beggar) | g | ___ | ___ |
| (foyer) | y | ___ | ___ | (hammer) | m | ___ | ___ | (paper) | p | ___ | ___ |
| (racket) | c, ck, k | ___ | ___ | (sweater) | t | ___ | ___ | (boxer) | x | ___ | ___ |
| (yellow) | l | ___ | ___ | (muffin) | f | ___ | ___ | (mohair) | h | ___ | ___ |

4. Initial consonant blends (Identifies initial blend from spoken word)

| | | | | | |
|---|---|---|---|---|---|
| sp-spare | ________ | tw-twill | ________ | bl-blare | ________ |
| st-stave | ________ | sw-swab | ________ | cl-clue | ________ |
| sl-sloth | ________ | fl-flinch | ________ | tr-troop | ________ |
| sm-smirk | ________ | sn-snob | ________ | br-brig | ________ |
| spr-spring | ________ | str-string | ________ | spl-split | ________ |
| gr-grime | ________ | cr-cram | ________ | fr-frill | ________ |
| dr-droll | ________ | | | | |

5. Final consonant blends (Identifies final blend from spoken word)

| | | | | | |
|---|---|---|---|---|---|
| st-waist | ________ | ck-lack | ________ | nd-wound | ________ |
| nt-cent | ________ | ng-bring | ________ | ld-shield | ________ |
| lt-stilt | ________ | mp-hump | ________ | nk-think | ________ |

6. Initial consonant digraphs (Identifies initial digraph from spoken word)

   sh-shin ______ wh-whistle ______ sh-show ______ th-then ______ ph-phantom ______

7. Final consonant digraphs (Identifies final digraph from spoken word)

   sh-wish ______ ch-pouch ______ th-birth ______ ph-graph ______

8. Long-vowel sound (Identifies final digraph from spoken word)

   (hate) a ______ (mete) e ______ (life) i ______ (cold) o ______ (mute) u ______

9. Short-vowel sounds (Identifies short vowel from spoken word)

   (add) a ______ (end) e ______ (kid) i ______ (not) o ______ (tub) u ______

10. Regular vowel combinations (Identifies regular vowel combination from spoken word)

    ee-sheet ______ ai-rain ______ oa-float ______ ay-spray ______ ea-peach ______

11. Irregular vowel combinations (Identifies irregular vowel combination from spoken word)

    ow, ou-trout ______ aw-awning ______ au-taught ______ ea-peach ______
    ie-lied ______ ew-crew ______ ow-crow ______ ea-head ______

12. Irregular phonetic parts (Identifies irregular phonetic part from spoken word)

    (character/chord) ck (k) ______ (quest) qu ______ (sigh) igh ______
    (scene) sc ______ (scholar) sch (sk) ______ (might) ight ______ (heart/shear) ear ______

13. Hard/soft letter sounds (Identifies hard/soft letter sounds from spoken word)

    (candy) hard c ______ (gather) hard g ______
    (circle) soft c ______ (giraffe) soft g ______

14. Diphthongs (Identifies diphthongs from spoken word)

    (tar) ar ______ (ploy) oy ______ (lord) or ______ (stir) ir ______
    (fur) ur ______ (fern) er ______ (moon) oo ______ (spoil) oi ______

15. Silent letters (Identifies silent letters from spoken word)

    (comb) b ______ (gnaw) g ______ (know) k ______

II. ____________ will prove competent in the following primary structural analysis skills.

1. Correct plural form (Selects correct form from printed choice'

| | | | |
|---|---|---|---|
| ball balls | ball balls | cat cats | cat cats |

OR

a. Ann plays with a ________________ .
(doll, dolls)

b. We have two ________________ .
(pet, pets)

c. There are seven ________________ in a week.
(day, days)

d. How many ________________ are in your town?
(church, churches)

Verb forms (Selects correct form from printed choice)

a. John ________________ ball.
(play, plays, playing)

b. Tom ________________ fast.
(runned, run, runs)

c. Ann ________________ to a new school.
(move, moving, moved)

d. The snow ________________ the ground.
(cover, covered, covering)

e. The rabbit ________________ up and down.
(hop, hopping, hopped)

f. He ________________ into the woods.
(heading, head, headed)

g. The children ________________ for the bus.
(waits, waiting, waited)

h. The rain ________________ yesterday.
(stops, stopped, stop)

i. The children are ________________ .
(sang, singing, sing)

j. The girls were ________________ along.
(skipping, skips, skipped)

3. Selects compound words from a list (into, playhouse, fireman, school, running, rabbit, yesterday, camper, sidewalk, grandfather)

4. Identifies rhymes

Directions: At least four words should be written after each.

dad ____________ will ____________ make ____________ pin ____________

5. Possessive forms

a. This is ________________ house.
(Jacks, Jack's)

b. The ____________ pan is lost.
(dog's, dogs)

c. Two ____________ bones were in the yard.
(dogs' dogs)

6. Comparative adjective forms

a. Jane is ________________ than John.
(fast, faster, fastest)

b. Mary is the ________________ girl in her class.
(thinner, thinnest)

c. Christmas is the ________________ time of the year.
(happier, happiest)

7. Verb forms

a. His arm was ________________.
(broke, broken)

b. Have you ________________ your spelling words?
(wrote, written)

c. He ________________ a cookie from the plate.
(took, taken)

## Note

In the next two goals, reading needs to be assessed in both quality and quantity. The following tips are offered to help teachers balance the objectives in reading with the normal grade expectations, to establish IEP goals.

While listening to oral reading, you may want to note omissions and additions, as well as the general decoding skills. Some teachers may collect old discarded reading series and make their own diagnostic kit. When having the student read orally, use 80 percent as a minimum acceptable level for mastery for word recognition.

Comprehension should be checked on both silent and oral reading by the use of questions. Following are the things to look for and the kinds of questions to ask at each grade level.

## Reading

*Primer.* Use the controlled vocabulary of any primer. Look for correct phrasing, easy word recognition, fluency, and some literal comprehension. Use 80 percent as the minimum for acceptable mastery.

*First.* Using standard first-grade material, have the student answer questions about *what, where,* and *when.* Look for accuracy of detail. Use 80 percent as the minimum for acceptable mastery.

*Second.* Use a second-grade basal reader or the *Gray Oral Reading Test* passages or other standardized reading diagnostic passages. In addition to word recognition and fluency, determine student's comprehension by asking for details and inference questions. Second-grade students should answer *why* questions. Use 80 percent as the minimum for acceptable mastery.

*Third.* Use a third-grade basal reader or a diagnostic reading kit. Consider 80 percent as minimum accuracy on recognition and comprehension. Student should answer *where, what,* and *why* questions, and be able to define any vocabulary word in a sentence.

*Fourth.* This is the last oral reading test, due to age factors. The student should read with great fluency, and listening should give other information and pleasure. Use 80 percent minimum criteria on word recognition; and, at this point, expect the student to draw conclusions, make inferences, and project endings.

*Fifth.* Check silent reading only. Look for more involved, longer passages. In addition to answering straight, detailed questions, the student should be able to answer questions to involve full explanation of an event in the passge. The student should also be able to answer questions about feelings and project alternatives (What if . . . ?). At level, student might be expected to summarize a passage in his own words.

*Sixth.* Students at this point should be reading for information and pleasure. Vocabulary should be challenging and allow students to develop advanced perception of events. This would include character interpretation, projection of future events, and summarizing information.

III. ______________ will prove competent at word recognition at following levels

Primer (Calls 16+ words correctly from list of 20 words)

| | | | | | | | |
|---|---|---|---|---|---|---|---|
| all | _____ | at | _____ | boat | _____ | but | _____ |
| do | _____ | duck | _____ | find | _____ | girl | _____ |
| he | _____ | kitten | _____ | like | _____ | now | _____ |
| out | _____ | put | _____ | saw | _____ | stop | _____ |
| thank | _____ | train | _____ | there | _____ | three | _____ |

First (Calls 16+ words correctly from list of 20 words)

| | | | | | | | |
|---|---|---|---|---|---|---|---|
| about | _____ | as | _____ | be | _____ | by | _____ |
| could | _____ | fast | _____ | friend | _____ | guess | _____ |
| hen | _____ | how | _____ | long | _____ | mitten | _____ |
| never | _____ | old | _____ | party | _____ | sat | _____ |
| some | _____ | tell | _____ | tree | _____ | walk | _____ |

Second (Calls 16+ words correctly from list of 20 words)

| | | | | | | | |
|---|---|---|---|---|---|---|---|
| across | _____ | balloon | _____ | best | _____ | burn | _____ |
| care | _____ | coat | _____ | dress | _____ | fire | _____ |
| gone | _____ | knew | _____ | miss | _____ | off | _____ |
| pig | _____ | right | _____ | shall | _____ | six | _____ |
| table | _____ | together | _____ | turn | _____ | wood | _____ |

Third (Calls 16+ words correctly from list of 20 words)

| | | | | | | | |
|---|---|---|---|---|---|---|---|
| able | _____ | block | _____ | child | _____ | daddy | _____ |
| edge | _____ | fix | _____ | half | _____ | Indian | _____ |
| lot | _____ | mind | _____ | north | _____ | pile | _____ |
| pour | _____ | rich | _____ | street | _____ | silver | _____ |
| squirrel | _____ | teeth | _____ | trap | _____ | watch | _____ |

Fourth (Calls 23+ words correctly from list of 25 words)

| | | | | | | | |
|---|---|---|---|---|---|---|---|
| automobile | _____ | pronounce | _____ | trail | _____ | frolicking | _____ |
| stinging | _____ | metal | _____ | southpaw | _____ | inquisitive | _____ |
| duty | _____ | hall | _____ | pell-mell | _____ | skimmed | _____ |
| demanded | _____ | socks | _____ | seal | _____ | magazine | _____ |
| remove | _____ | musicians | _____ | crawling | _____ | terror | _____ |
| nuisance | _____ | crash | _____ | iron | _____ | natural | _____ |
| delivered | _____ | | | | | | |

Fifth (Calls 23+ words correctly from list of 25 words)

| | | | | | | | |
|---|---|---|---|---|---|---|---|
| depending | _____ | welcome | _____ | surrounded | _____ | ambulances | _____ |
| proper | _____ | puppet | _____ | experience | _____ | quit | _____ |
| keen | _____ | freeze | _____ | nimble | _____ | sedan | _____ |
| possess | _____ | shirk | _____ | cloak | _____ | handcuffed | _____ |
| skating | _____ | border | _____ | statues | _____ | drooping | _____ |
| nursery | _____ | homestead | _____ | legends | _____ | pint | _____ |
| madam | _____ | | | | | | |

Sixth (Calls 23+ words correctly from list of 25 words)

| | | | | | | | |
|---|---|---|---|---|---|---|---|
| parachuting | _____ | create | _____ | miniature | _____ | hiking | _____ |
| brows | _____ | retorted | _____ | carton | _____ | precisely | _____ |
| obtained | _____ | mixture | _____ | flushed | _____ | appreciate | _____ |
| crusade | _____ | distressing | _____ | offense | _____ | updraft | _____ |
| passenger | _____ | infinite | _____ | structure | _____ | calico | _____ |
| gait | _____ | cathedral | _____ | woodpeckers | _____ | jumbled | _____ |
| cluttered | _____ | | | | | | |

IV. Oral Reading

_____________ will prove competent at oral reading while utilizing the following skills at appropriate grade level:

| | | | |
|---|---|---|---|
| reads 80% of words correctly | __________ | uses proper inflection | __________ |
| correct phrasing | __________ | reads with expression | __________ |
| correct posture | __________ | reads clearly and distinctly | __________ |
| reacts to punctuation | __________ | reads fluently | __________ |

V. Oral Reading Comprehension—Silent Reading Comprehension

_____________ will prove competent at comprehending oral and silent reading by demonstrating the following skills at appropriate level:

| | O | S | | O | S |
|---|---|---|---|---|---|
| recalls what has been read | ___ | ___ | follows printed directions | ___ | ___ |
| locates answers | ___ | ___ | understands symbols represent objects | ___ | ___ |
| reads to obtain answer | ___ | ___ | recalls what has been read silently | ___ | ___ |
| draws conclusion from given fact | ___ | ___ | associates test with picture | ___ | ___ |
| verifies a statement | ___ | ___ | sequences events | ___ | ___ |
| finds proof | ___ | ___ | draws conclusions | ___ | ___ |
| finds the main idea | ___ | ___ | predicts outcomes | ___ | ___ |
| finds specific information | ___ | ___ | finds main idea | ___ | ___ |
| uses page number and titles | ___ | ___ | obtains general information | ___ | ___ |
| recognizes emotional reactions | ___ | ___ | discriminates visual stimuli via descriptive words | ___ | ___ |
| finds cause and effect | ___ | ___ | finds details | ___ | ___ |
| sees relationships | ___ | ___ | makes inferential projections | ___ | ___ |
| finds support information | ___ | ___ | identifies the mood of selection | ___ | ___ |
| selects facts to support main idea | ___ | ___ | verifies answers | ___ | ___ |
| reads for definite purpose | ___ | ___ | summarizes story in own words | ___ | ___ |
| verifies, answers, opinion, hypothesis | ___ | ___ | interprets descriptive words | ___ | ___ |
| makes inferences | ___ | ___ | selects facts to remember | ___ | ___ |
| interprets feelings and attitudes | ___ | ___ | | | |

## VII. Vocabulary Expansion

_______________ will prove competent on the following vocabulary language skills at appropriate level:

| | O | S |
|---|---|---|
| defines multiple meaning of words (e.g., run, head, ship, can, etc.) | ____ | ____ |
| supplies synonyms (e.g., big, funny, thin, couch, blizzard, etc.) | ____ | ____ |
| supplies antonyms (e.g., soft, clean, first, found, etc.) | ____ | ____ |
| uses correct homonyms (e.g., mail, male; to, too, two; etc.) | ____ | ____ |

## VIII. Structural Analysis

_______________ will prove competent in the following intermediate structural analysis skills:

| | O | S |
|---|---|---|
| Recognizes prefixes (e.g., un, be, re, in, dis, pre, etc.) | ____ | ____ |
| Recognizes suffixes (e.g., ly, er, ward, ful, ness, etc.) | ____ | ____ |

Forms/uses irregular plurals

f to ves: leaf ___________, shelf ___________, knife ___________, calf ___________
stays the same: deer ___________, sheep ___________, fish ___________
changes form: ox ___________, woman ___________, child ___________

Forms/uses comparative and superlative adjective forms

er, est: ___________, stronger, strongest
y to i, add er, est: happy, ___________ happiest
changes form: ___________, better, best ___________, worse, ___________
more, most: ___________, more beautiful, most beautiful

Forms/uses verb tenses

Regular forms: ___________, helped, will help
Irregular forms: lead, ___________ will lead
go, went, ___________
___________ was, will be
___________, drove, will drive

Locates pronoun referents from a selection (e.g., who is he, it, etc.)
Defines meanings of prefixes (e.g., ab, bi, an, ante, etc.)
Defines meanings of suffixes (e.g., able, an, ence, hood, etc.)

## IX. Study Skills

_______________ will prove competence with study skills by demonstrating the following skills:

1. Locates information in appropriate source

| | | | |
|---|---|---|---|
| dictionary | ______ | encyclopedia | ______ |
| glossary | ______ | table of contents | ______ |

2. Use dictionary

| | | | |
|---|---|---|---|
| by first letter | ______ | by third letter | ______ |
| by second letter | ______ | by fourth letter | ______ |
| guide words | ______ | pronunciation key | ______ |
| definition | ______ | synonym | ______ |
| diacritical marking | ______ | | |

3. Classifies and categorizes

   vegetables ______ toys ______ furniture ______ vehicles ______ tools ______

4. Uses a map

| | | | |
|---|---|---|---|
| determines N-S-E-W | ______ | locate specific buildings | ______ |
| locate name of roads | ______ | comparative judgment | ______ |

5. Uses context clues for closure
6. Makes judgmental decisions (e.g., fact, fiction)
7. Outlines

| | | | |
|---|---|---|---|
| extract main idea | ______ | list of subordinate ideas | ______ |

APPENDIX TWO

# Glossary

1. Active Teaching — The interaction between teacher and pupil that indicates that the student is a participant in the lesson, and in which the teacher, through a variety of methods and materials, teaches a concept that will have application to academic tasks that will be assigned independently.
2. ADD — Attention Deficit Disorder
3. Advocate — A person or group committed to work for the benefit of special persons or groups. Currently, advocates have been active in advancing the cause of special education. This includes political action, lobbying, task forces, oversight committees, surrogate parenting, and other positive activities.
4. Baseline Data — After completing specialized observations, the information gathered is graphed according to frequency, consistency, etc. The data become a starting point for program planning.
5. Behavioral Data — Behavioral always means observable; therefore, behavioral data must be capable of being seen. This is an extremely important concept in education since it requires special language in framing learning objectives and plans.
6. Checklists — A lift of academic skills that are deemed necessary for mastery of academic subject matter.
7. Contingency Plans — A set of plans appropriate for one day for a given classroom that contain activities, spiritmaster worksheets, and alternative assignments that are independent of

ongoing teacher plans (should include activities that are fun).

8. Decoding — The act of analyzing a word phonetically or configuratively and thus being able to "make out" or say the word.
9. DDM — Document of Decision Making
10. Due Process — The law that gives every exceptional child protection for receiving the most appropriate educational program possible.
11. EMR — A term used in referring to educable mentally retarded individuals.
12. Entitlement — Those programs that a citizen is deemed to own as a right, to be provided by government.
13. ESY — Extended School Year
14. Functioning Level — The academic level at which a student is performing independently.
15. FAPE — Free Appropriate Public Education
16. FERPA — Family Education Rights and Privacy Act
17. Hierarchy — An ordering that goes from top to bottom with logical structure. Used in education to develop programming and design special curricula.
18. IDEA — Individuals with Disabilities Educational Act (formerly PL94-142).
19. IEP — An individualized education plan tailored for each child's unique problems and needs.
20. Inclusive Education/Encoding — Peer sensitivity to facilitate integration of handicapped students with age appropriate peers.
21. Interagency Council — Use of multi agencies as a team to make decisions for a child's program.
22. LD — A term used in referring to children with learning disabilities.
23. LDA — Learning Disabilities Association of America (formerly ACLD). A national organization to further the cause for persons who have specific problems.
24. Mediator — Independent third party who tries to resolve differences.
25. MDT — Multi-Discipline Team
26. LEA — Local education agency. The local education unit for organizing and recommending for a special child. Must include the regular teacher, special teacher, school psychologist, speech therapist or speech clinician, and other knowledgeable professionals.
27. Learning Center — An area set apart where a student goes to do a specific activity characterized by highly motivating materials,

manipulatives, and other unique approaches.

28. Learning Mode — Theoretically, the concept that learning is best accomplished by one or another sensory channel. Visual mode would indicate that the learner recalls information best when it is presented visually. Auditory mode would mean that the learner takes verbal input best, and tactile would describe a need to "feel information" through touch.

29. LRE — Least restrictive environment is a prominent concept of IDEA (PL94-142). This mandates that handicapped children shall not be separated from their normal peers unnecessarily. Accommodations must be made to include handicapped children with their peers whenever possible and to separate them only when they are being served in a special way.

30. Mandate — Required by law and therefore not optional for school districts or professionals. People frequently refer to federal or state mandates, which are not always the same. (This really means a legal requirement.)

31. NORA — Notice of Recommended Assignment (Due Process Document)

32. OCR — Office of Civil Rights

33. OSEP — Office of Special Education Education Programs

34. OVR — Office of Vocational Rehabilitation

35. PEL — Present Education Level

36. Pendency — Child stays in current placement until issue is resolved.

37. Perception — The process of sensory input and integrating it into meaningful cognitive information. Visual, auditory, tactile, kinesthetic, etc.

38. PL94-142 — The federal legislation which mandates a free and appropriate individualized educational program for every exceptional child, now called IDEA (Individuals with Disabilities Educational Act).

39. PL99-457 — Preschool law effective 1991

40. Prescription — An individualized program based on a full assessment of the child's strengths and weaknesses.

41. Psychological Test — A test given by a person trained in testing (a psychologist, a psychometrist). IQ tests are usually referred to as psychologicals.

42. Reading Comprehension — The act of understanding written language and making meaningful sense out of what has been read or heard. This usually involves relating the read material to material previously learned or experienced.

| | |
|---|---|
| 43. Remand | To return—send back |
| 44. S & EM or S & ED | A term denoting children with social and emotional maladjustment problems. |
| 45. Sensory Data | Information a person takes in through the senses. In education this is usually restricted to visual (eyes), auditory (ears), and tactile (touch). |
| 46. Student Management Approaches | Positive reinforcement: Teacher recognizes and rewards specific incidences of good behavior based on the theoretical assumption that it will occur with greater frequency once it is rewarded.<br>Negative reinforcement: The act of punishing specific incidences, or removing previously given rewards in an effort to limit behavior and reduce the probability of reoccurrences.<br>Contingency management: The process of contracting in advance for specific behaviors in exchange for specific rewards.<br>Modeling: The act of demonstrating and calling attention to desired behavior or pointing to desired behavior in another. |
| 47. TMR | A term used to denote individuals who are trainable mentally retarded. |

APPENDIX THREE

# Sample IEPs

Instruction Area: Language Arts | Student's Name: Sheree | School Year

Annual Goal: Sheree will develop receptive language skills

*Short-Term Objective*

| *Educational Tasks* | *Evaluation Procedures/Conditions* | *Success Criteria* | *Progress* |
|---|---|---|---|
| Will follow verbal directions up to 4 commands | Tape recorder, teacher observation | 85% on 3 trials | |
| Will identify nonsense | Tape recorder, teacher observation | 85% on 3 trials | |
| Will classify and categorize given topics | Teacher worksheets | 85% on 2 trials | |

Instructional Area: Language Arts | Student's Name: Sheree | School Year

Annual Goal: Sherree will develop expressive language skills

*Short-Term Objective*

| *Educational Tasks* | *Evaluation Procedures/Conditions* | *Success Criteria* | *Progress* |
|---|---|---|---|
| Will improve cursive handwriting skills | Teacher worksheets | 90% on 3 trials | |
| Will write sentences using correct word order | Teacher worksheets | 90% on 3 trials | |
| Will identify telling and asking questions | Commercial and teacher worksheets | 85% on 3 trials | |

Instructional Area: Math | Student's Name: Sheree | School Year

Annual Goal: Sheree will improve use of functional math terms

*Short-Term Objective*

| *Educational tasks* | *Evaluation Procedures/Conditions* | *Success Criteria* | *Progress* |
|---|---|---|---|
| Will recognize and name the following signs: \$, ¢, X, greater than and less than | Teacher worksheet | 85% accuracy on 3 trials | |
| Will recognize and name the fractions: one half, one third, and three fourths | Teacher worksheet and teacher observation | 85% accuracy on 3 trials | |
| Will create the following fractions: one half, one third, and three fourths | Teacher observation | 90% accuracy on 2 trials | |

Instructional Area: Math | Student's Name: Sheree | School Year

Annual Goal: Sheree will demonstrate application of skills of calendar, time, and money

*Short-Term Objective*

| *Educational Tasks* | *Evaluation Procedures/Conditions* | *Success Criteria* | *Progress* |
|---|---|---|---|
| Will write and name the months of the year | Teacher observation | 85% accuracy on 3 trials | |
| Will tell and convert clock time to the hour, half hour, and quarter hour | Clock, teacher observation | 85% accuracy on daily trials in 1 week | |
| Will convert and use money | Real money; teacher observation | 85% accuracy on daily trials in 1 week | |

Instructional Area: Behavior | Student's Name: Jeff | School Year

Annual Goal: Jeff will improve his in-seat behavior

*Short-Term Objective*

| *Educational Tasks* | *Evaluation Procedures* | *Success Criteria* | *Progress* |
|---|---|---|---|
| Jeff will remain in his seat during direct instruction. | Jeff will be placed on a 5-minute verbal reinforcement schedule | 80% of instructional period | |
| Jeff will reduce his peer instruction. | Jeff will be on a token system "for not bothering his neighbors." | 50% reduction of pupil-pupil interaction over base line frequency. | |

Instructional Area: Math | Student's Name: Kim | School Year

Annual Goal: Kim will be able to apply math concepts

*Short-Term Objective*

| *Educational Tasks* | *Evaluation Procedures/Conditions* | *Success Criteria* | *Progress* |
|---|---|---|---|
| Kim will solve word problems involving addition, subtraction, multiplication, or division. | Unit tests | 70% accuracy | |
| Kim will make change, given the cost of the purchases and money available. | 10 making-change problems | 80% accuracy | |
| Kim will tell and write time in notation form, e.g., 6:45. | Kim will tell the time for 5 o'clock and write the time for 5 clocks. | 80% accuracy | |

Instructional Area: Social Studies and Science | Student's Name: Mark | School Year

Annual Goal: Mark will be integrated in the regular tenth-grade Social Studies and Science classes with the following modification in the LD room:

*Short-Term Objective*

| *Educational Tasks* | *Evaluation Procedures/Conditions* | *Success Criteria* | *Progress* |
|---|---|---|---|
| 1. Mark will have materials reinterpreted upon registration | Regular education grading | Regular grading criteria | |
| 2. Drill sheets will be done in the LD room | Regular education grading | Regular grading criteria | |
| 3. All study guides be reviewed with the LD teacher | Regular education grading | Regular grading criteria | |
| 4. All tests will be administered in the LD room | Regular education grading | Regular grading criteria | |
| 5. Special projects will be contracted by LD teacher to expand grade (e.g., manipulations) | Contract | Contract | |

Instructional Area: Study Skills | Student's Name: Mark | School Year

Annual Goal: Mark will improve competence with study skills by demonstrating the following skills:

*Short-Term Objective*

| *Educational Tasks* | *Evaluation Procedures/Conditions* | *Success Criteria* | *Progress* |
|---|---|---|---|
| 1. Locate information in the appropriate source (e.g., dictionary, index, etc.) | Given a choice, Mark will correctly select:<br>a. dictionary (spelling)<br>b. encyclopedia (background)<br>c. telephone directory (address)<br>for information | 100% accuracy | |
| 2. Locate local area using map coordinator | Outline of chapter in Social Studies | Correct main idea and 80% supporting data | |

Instructionsl Area: Math | Student's Name: Mark | School Year

Annual Goal: Mark will prove competent with the following percentage skills:

Short-Term Objective

| Educational Tasks | Evaluation Procedures/Conditions | Success Criteria | Progress |
|---|---|---|---|
| 1. Mark will recognize percentages | Regular text | 100% accuracy | |
| 2. Mark will convert baseball scores to decimals | Teacher-made worksheet | 80% accuracy | |
| 3. Mark will compute percentage for word problems | Hayes worksheet | 80% accuracy | |

Instructional Area: Reading | Student's Name: Mark | School Year

Annual Goal: Mark will prove competent at silent reading skills by demonstrating the following skills:

Short-Term Objective

| Educational Tasks | Evaluation Procedures/Conditions | Success Criteria | Progress |
|---|---|---|---|
| 1. Follows printed directions | Completed worksheet | 80% accuracy | |
| 2. Identifies the mood of a selection | Labels a story end: happy, suspenseful, etc. | 100% accuracy | |
| 3. Recognizes character traits | Describes characters and motivation of each | Reasonable interpretation | |
| 4. Summarizes selection | Teacher judgment | Concise summary | |

Instructional Area: Language | Student's Name: Mark | School Year

Annual Goal: Mark will prove competent at the following functional language skills:

Short-Term Objective

| Educational Tasks | Evaluation Procedures/Conditions | Success Criteria | Progress |
|---|---|---|---|
| 1. Identifies and uses appropriate abbreviations for months, days of week, measurement forms, and forms of address | Teacher-made worksheets | 80% accuracy | |
| 2. Identifies similarities and metaphors | Selects and explains from literary selection | Teacher judgment | |

Instructional Area: Language | Student's Name: Scott | School Year

Annual Goal: Scott will develop functional language skills.

Short-Term Objective

| Educational Tasks | Evaluation Procedures/Conditions | Success Criteria | Progress |
|---|---|---|---|
| 1. Receptive/integration: Follows verbal directions | Given a set of commands using a checklist | 80% accuracy | |
| 2. Written language skills: | | | |
| Will write legibly | Given a daily assignment | 80% accuracy | |
| Spells selected sight words | Given a list of sight words | 80% accuracy | |

Short-Term Objective

Instructional Area: Language | Student's Name: Scott | School Year

Annual Goal: Scott will develop functional language skills

| *Educational Tasks* | *Evaluation Procedures/Conditions* | *Success Criteria* | *Progress* |
|---|---|---|---|
| 1. Preposition, conjunction, interjection | Grizzard book page | 80% accuracy | |
| 2. Use correct verb forms | Our American Language | 80% accuracy | |
| 3. Write and use outline | Teacher worksheet | 80% accuracy | |
| 4. Write exposition paragraph from outline | Teacher worksheet | 80% accuracy | |
| 5. Recognize and read and complete analogies | Continental Press sheet | 80% accuracy | |

Short-Term Objective

Instructional Area: Reading | Student's Name: Scott | School Year

Annual Goal: Scott will develop reading skills.

| *Educational Tasks* | *Evaluation Procedures/Conditions* | *Success Criteria* | *Progress* |
|---|---|---|---|
| 1. Will develop primary structural analysis skills<br>Selects/produces correct verb form | Given choice of verb forms | 80% accuracy | |

Instructional Area LANGUAGE IEP Conference Date ______ Student's Name KELLY

Present Level of Educational Performance Kelly produces non-speech sounds through-out the day. She frequently produces vowels like sounds. Kelly responds to sound stimulation by vocalizing. This has been noted by parents and teachers.

Annual Goal To improve both receptive and expressive language skills.

Short Term Objectives

| Educational Task(s) | Evaluation Procedures/Conditions | Success Criteria | Progress |
|---|---|---|---|
| 1. During regular school day Kelly will look and/or vocalize when her name is called. | Teacher and/or aide observation when verbal cues or physical prompts are initiated. | At least two thirds of the time consistently. | |
| 2. During daily activities Kelly will continue to respond to vocal stimulation. | After ample response time at least a fifty percent response as observed by teacher and/or aide. | Continuing increasing response to vocal stimulation (directed) | |
| 3. During daily activities Kelly reacts and coos when music is turned on. | Observation of cooing and/or other reaction when stimulus is presented via tapes, radio or records. | Observation of target behavior. | |

Teacher Comments

Progress Key: (M) mastered (P) progressing (NI) not introduced (N) needs remediation
(S) frustration (R) regression (ESY) extended school year

Copies to: Official File (white) Teacher File (yellow) District Office File (pink) Parent (goldenrod)

Instructional Area COGNITIVE IEP Conference Date ______ Student's Name VALERIE

Present Level of Educational Performance according to a therapist observation and parent report, Valerie brings her feet and hands to her mouth in a playful, exploratory manner. She responds to loud sounds by turning her head and quieting her behavior. Valerie manipulates objects with her left hand in repetitive patterns. She can remove objects from a container when directed.

Annual Goal Increase manual exploration, visual and auditory attention to objects and people.

Short Term Objectives

| Educational Task(s) | Evaluation Procedures/Conditions | Success Criteria | Progress |
|---|---|---|---|
| 1. Given an interesting toy or object, Valerie will attend and respond. | Teacher and/or aide will chart behavior during directed activity | 3 to 4 minutes of attentive responding. | |
| 2. Given a simple battery - operated or cause effect toy, Valerie will activate with consistent motor behavior. | After guidance and physical prompts - active play with a toy for 2 to 5 minutes consistently | Observed "play" | |
| 3. Given a variety of toys to play with, and physical prompts Valerie will perform at least three different actions with the object in play. | Action such as shaking, banging and pulling will be observed after instruction. | 70% of the time when toys are presented or available. | |
| 4. Given blocks and a container, Valerie will drop the blocks in upon verbal prompt. | Obedience to direction (Drop It) | 5 times out of 6 on verbal cue. | |

Teacher Comments

Progress Key: (M) mastered (P) progressing (NI) not introduced (N) needs remediation (S) frustration (R) regression (ESY) extended school year

Copies to: Official File (white) Teacher File (yellow) District Office File (pink) Parent (goldenrod)

Instructional Area: Vocational Training  IEP Conference Date: ______  Student's Name: Ryan L.

Present Level of Educational Performance: Ryan is quick when working with hands-on material. He routinely takes apart and re-assembles appliances and toys.

His reading level is mid third grade and math level is beginning fourth grade. Ryan has little interest in academics. He is enthusiastic about all aspects of automobiles.

Annual Goal: Ryan will identify and use tools properly.

Short Term Objectives

| Educational Task(s) | Evaluation Procedures/Conditions | Success Criteria | Progress |
|---|---|---|---|
| 1. Ryan will identify tools by name | Oral quiz | 90% | |
| 2. Ryan will read and write the names of tools (labeling) | Vocabulary test based on pictures | 75% | |
| 3. Ryan will match the correct tool to standard usage | Class discussion<br>Lab demonstration | 85% | |

Teacher Comments

Progress Key: (M) mastered (P) progressing (NI) not introduced (N) needs remediation
(S) frustration (R) regression (ESY) extended school year

Copies to: Official File (white), Teacher File (yellow), District Office File (pink), Parent (goldenrod)

Instructional Area **Vocational Training** IEP Conference Date ______ Student's Name **Ryan L.**

Present Level of Educational Performance

SEE PAGE 1

Annual Goal **Will be competent with automotive measuring skills**

Short Term Objectives.

| Educational Task(s) | Evaluation Procedures/Conditions | Success Criteria | Progress |
|---|---|---|---|
| 1. Ryan will identify automotive measuring tools | Teacher observation | 95% | |
| 2. Ryan will use appropriate terminology | Quiz- oral<br>written | 85% | |
| 3. Ryan will demonstrate correct measurement on liquid, weight, linear, and pressure | Use and recording from appropriate instruments | 90% | |
| 4. Read tool measurements correctly | Reads tire guage, micrometer, wrench fractions | 95% | |

Teacher Comments

Progress Key: (M) mastered (P) progressing (NI) not introduced (N) needs remediation
(S) frustration (R) regression (ESY) extended school year

Copies to: Official File (white) District Office File (pink)
Teacher File (yellow) Parent (goldenrod)

STUDENT NAME NATHAN MASH DOB 5/20/78 Date 9/20/92

INSTRUCTIONAL AREA(S) BEHAVIOR

PRESENT LEVELS OF EDUCATIONAL PERFORMANCE Nathan is very intelligent; needs structure and classroom breaks. His main problem seems to be an Attention Deficit Disorder (ADD).

SPECIALLY DESIGNED INSTRUCTION A classroom behavior point system coupled with a reduction of distractible stimuli. Ten minutes of independent on-task behavior to be reinforced with teacher-aide instructional attention.

ANNUAL GOAL(S) Nathan will improve in the following behavioral skills following assessment:

| SHORT-TERM INSTRUCTIONAL OBJECTIVES | ASSESSMENT PROCEDURES | SCHEDULE OF ASSESSMENT | CRITERIA FOR SUCCESS | PROGRESS/ LEARNING OUTCOME |
|---|---|---|---|---|
| Will demonstrate a more positive attitude toward self<br>----describing feelings<br>----making positive statements about self<br>----participating in group discussions<br>----demonstrating self-care | | | | |

PLANNED COURSES FOR ALL CURRICULAR AREAS ARE AVAILABLE UPON REQUEST

Progress Key: (M) mastered (P) progressing (NI) not introduced (N) needs remediation (S) frustration (R) regression

Copies to: Official File (white) District (pink) Teacher File (yellow) Parent (goldenrod)

STUDENT NAME NATHAN MASH DOB 5/20/78 Date 9/20/92

INSTRUCTIONAL AREA(S) BEHAVIOR

PRESENT LEVELS OF EDUCATIONAL PERFORMANCE Nathan is very intelligent; needs structure and monitored classroom breaks. His main problem seems to be an Attention Deficit Disorder (ADD).

SPECIALLY DESIGNED INSTRUCTION A classroom behavior point system coupled with a reduction of distractible stimuli, and a highly structured series of 10 minute teaching sessions followed by reinforced independent work.

ANNUAL GOAL(S) Nathan will improve in the following behavioral skills following assessment:

| SHORT-TERM INSTRUCTIONAL OBJECTIVES | ASSESSMENT PROCEDURES | SCHEDULE OF ASSESSMENT | CRITERIA FOR SUCCESS | PROGRESS/ LEARNING OUTCOME |
|---|---|---|---|---|
| Will follow school and classroom rules<br>----following schedule<br>----attending regularly<br>----being on time<br>----maintaining organization<br>----responding to authority figures<br>----seeking help appropriately<br>----using appropriate language | | | | |

PLANNED COURSES FOR ALL CURRICULAR AREAS ARE AVAILABLE UPON REQUEST

Progress Key: (M) mastered (P) progressing (NI) not introduced (N) needs remediation (S) frustration (R) regression

Copies to: Official File (white) Teacher File (yellow) District (pink) Parent (goldenrod)

## APPENDIX FOUR

# Teacher's Master Schedules
# Student's Weekly Schedules
# Student's Daily Schedules

# Teacher's Master Schedules

Pages 107-111 demonstrate an actual weekly schedule for one teacher. As shown, each day of the week has been done separately. Within each day, the time segments are listed on the vertical axis. Across the top, the name of each student appears. The general configuration of every day is outlined. The specifics, of course, will be in the daily lesson plans.

Pages 112-113 show a different type of planning. Page 112 outlines those times when the teacher will be working with resource secondary students. The vertical axis represents the periods of the day, and the horizontal axis is divided into the five days of the week. Individual blocks show who is in the room or which room the teacher is in with her LD students.

Page 113 shows where her students are when they are not with her.

Page 114 is a simple model. It divides the day into periods on the vertical axis, the days of the week across the horizontal axis, and then lists the names of students that will be in the room in each block. This is, perhaps, the most flexible schedule since it does not tie the teacher down to any given subject, but it requires more extensive planning via daily lesson plans.

Page 115 serves a slightly different purpose. It is instructionally orienteu and is prepared weekly. It can be used to list teaching objectives from the IEP for a week's work and serves more as a master plan than as a schedule. It is included since it is an excellent organizational tool.

Another helpful instructional tool is the weekly academic plan on Page 116. This form is used by teachers who plan by students rather than by time and is another signpost to original IEP goals. Long-range goals are placed under weekly objectives while short-range tasks are filled in daily. This form allows a teacher to reteach or review based on what is accomplished daily. Maintained in a loose-leaf notebook, it can be the most highly accountable document in a student's file.

Page 117 is a highly specific teaching schedule prepared by one teacher. The specificity is a supervisor's dream, but this type of scheduling requires constant modification and few teachers are willing to give up the time necessary to do it.

Page 118 is a sample of one-day scheduling in a resource room while the format is simple examination and shows this to be a highly comprehensive schedule. Since this must be done for five different days and modified weekly, it is really time consuming, but an excellent format.

Many teachers use the initials of a program or workbook for a student. In addition, students quickly learn "teacher shorthand," such as R for reading, M for math, etc. Each code is very personalized and highly idiosyncratic.

Monday

| | | 3rd | | | 4th | | | 5th | | | | 6th | | |
|---|---|---|---|---|---|---|---|---|---|---|---|---|---|---|
| | Bob | Bill | Dave | Ruth | Matt | Kim | Rick | Tara | Don | Tina | | Ed | | |
| 9:10 9:30 | 2 | BARNELL LOFT | SRA | READING INTEC | 6 | 3 | RHW | 4 | MATH INTEC | 1 | | R | | |
| 9:30 9:50 | MHW | R | R | | R | 1 | SRA | SRA | | 6 | | 9:45 | | |
| 9:50 10:10 | 6 | RHW | RHW | | RHW | R | R | 1 | 10:05 | SRA | | P.E. | | |
| 10:10 10:30 | 3 | MATH | 6 | SRA | 2 | RHW | RHW | M | 1 | M | | 10:15 BARNELL | | |
| 10:30 10:50 | MUSIC | | 2 | M | 1 | 6 | 1 | MHW | SRA | MHW | | LOFT RHW | | |
| 10:50 11:10 | 11:05 | 3 | 1 | MHW | SRA | M | M | 10:55 | | | | MHW 11:00 | | |
| 11:10 11:30 | R | MUSIC | MUSIC | MUSIC | MUSIC | MUSIC | 6 | 11:25 GYM | GYM | GYM | | MATH INTEC | | |
| 11:30 12:10 | A | 2 | M | 1 | M | A | MHW | SCIENCE 12:15 | SCIENCE | SCIENCE | | 12 | | |
| 12:10 1:10 | | | | L | U | N | C | H | | | | | | |
| 1:10 1:30 | WRITING | SS | SS | SS | SS | SS | SS | R | A | A | | | | |
| 1:30 1:50 | | | | | | | | A | R | R | | | | |
| 1:50 2:10 | MATH INTEG. | | | | 5 | A | AIDE | RHW | RHW | RHW | | | | |
| 2:10 2:30 | | A | A | A | A | S | | SS | SS | SS | | | | |
| 2:30 2:50 | A | S | S | S | S | MHW | MHW | | | | | | | |
| 2:50 3:10 | S | | SCIENCE | SCIENCE | SCIENCE | SCIENCE | SCIENCE | | | | | | | |
| 3:10 3:30 | 1 | | 3:45 | | | | | 3:00 AIDE S | S | S | | | | |
| | | | | | | | | | | | | | | |

Tuesday

| | 3rd | | | | 4th | | | 5th | | | 6th | | |
|---|---|---|---|---|---|---|---|---|---|---|---|---|---|
| | Bob | Bill | DAVE | RUTH | MATT | KIM | RICK | TARA | DON | TINA | | Ed | | |
| 9:10<br>9:30 | RHW | SHW | MHW | READ INTEG | MHW | L | L | SHW | SHW | 2 | | 1 | | |
| 9:30<br>9:50 | 3 | 1 | | ↓ | 1 | LHW | 4 | M | 2 | M | | SRH | | |
| 9:50<br>10:10 | ↓ | R | R | ↓ | R | 1 | BARNELL LOFT | 6<br>10:00 | BARNELL LOFT | BARNELL LOFT | | BARNELL LOFT | | |
| 10:10<br>10:30 | ↓ | MATH<br>↓ | 1 | SHW | 6 | R | R | ↓<br>SCIENCE | ↓<br>SC | ↓<br>SC | | ART | | |
| 10:30<br>10:50 | ↓<br>10:40 | ↓ | RHW | M | RHW | 5 | RHW | 1 | 6 | SHW | | ↓ | | |
| 10:50<br>11:10 | 6 | RHW | SHW | MHW | SHW | M | M | 2 | RED READING BK | BARNELL LOFT | | ↓ | | |
| 11:10<br>11:30 | R | SS | SS | SS | SS | SS | SS | SS | SS | SS | | MATH INTEG | | |
| 11:30<br>12:10 | A | A | MISS M | A | M | RHW | ↓<br>A | ↓<br>12:00 | ↓ | ↓ | | ↓<br>12:00 | | |
| 12:10<br>1:10 | | | | L | U | N | C | H | | | | | | |
| 1:10<br>1:30 | | SC | SCIENCE | SCIENCE | SCIENCE | SCIENCE | SCIENCE | A | R | R | | SS | | |
| 1:30<br>1:50 | | ↓ | ↓ | ↓ | ↓ | ↓ | ↓ | BARNELL LOFT | MATH BACK UP | A | | ↓ | | |
| 1:50<br>2:10 | MATH INTEG | ↓<br>L | ↓<br>1:55 | ↓<br>L | ↓<br>L | ↓<br>A | ↓<br>SHW | MUSIC<br>↓ | MUSIC | MUSIC | | ↓ | | |
| 2:10<br>2:30 | 2:15 | | | | | | | ↓<br>12:15 | | AIDE | | R | | |
| 2:30<br>2:50 | A | GYM | GYM | GYM | GYM | GYM | GYM | MHW<br>A | | 1 | | L | | |
| 2:50<br>3:10 | RHW | ↓ | ↓ | ↓ | ↓ | ↓ | ↓ | R | MATH INTEG<br>3:15 | A | | 3:00<br>SCIENCE | | |
| 3:10<br>3:30 | SHW | LHW | LHW | LHW | LHW | SHW | LHW | L | L | L | | ↓ | | |
| | | | | | | | | | | | | ↓<br>3:45 | | |

*Wednesday*

| | | 3rd | | 4th | | | 5th | | 6th | | | | | |
|---|---|---|---|---|---|---|---|---|---|---|---|---|---|---|
| | Bob | Bill | DAVE | Ruth | MATT | KIM | Rick | TARA | DON | TINA | | Ed | | |
| 9:10<br>9:30 | P.E.. | S | MHW | READ<br>INTEG | MHW | 1 | MHW | BARNELL<br>LOFT | MATH<br>INTEG | RHW | | R | | |
| 9:30<br>9:50 | ↓<br>9:40 | R | R | ↓ | R | MHW | 1 | | ↓ | 3 | | SRA<br>9:45 | | |
| 9:50<br>10:10 | LHW | RHW | RHW | ↓ | RHW | R | R | | ↓<br>10:05 | MHW | | P.E. | | |
| 10:10<br>10:30 | 6 | MATH | 3 | 2 | 1 | CHW | RHW | M | RHW | M | | 10:15<br>LHW | | |
| 10:30<br>10:50 | WRITING | ↓ | BARNELL<br>LOFT | M | 3 | 6 | 2 | MHW | 1 | MHW | | 5<br>BARNELL | | |
| 10:50<br>11:10 | 5 | 4 | 1 | MHW | BARNELL<br>LOFT | M | M | 10:55 | | | | LOFT<br>11:00 | | |
| 11:10<br>11:30 | R | SS | SS | SS | SS | SS | GYM | GYM | | | | MATH<br>REG<br>CLASS | | |
| 11:30<br>12:10 | L | ↓ | ↓ | ↓ | ↓ | ↓ | ↓ | ↓<br>SCIENCE | | | | ↓<br>12:00 | | |
| 12:10<br>1:10 | | | | L | U | N | C | H | | | | | | |
| 1:10<br>1:30 | WRITING | SC. | SCIENCE | SCIENCE | SCIENCE | SCIENCE | SC. | R | A | | | | | |
| 1:30<br>1:50 | 1:35<br>↓ | ↓ | ↓ | ↓ | ↓ | ↓ | ↓ | A | R | | | | | |
| 1:50<br>2:10 | MATH<br>INTEG | BARNELL | 1:55<br>4 | 1 | MHW | MHW | | A | A | | | | | |
| 2:10<br>2:30 | ↓<br>2:15 | A | A | A | A | S | S | SS | SS | | | | | |
| 2:30<br>2:50 | A | S | S | S | S | A | A | ↓ | ↓ | | | | | |
| 2:50<br>3:10 | S | ART | ART | ART | ART | ART | | ↓<br>3:00 | ↓ | | | | | |
| 3:10<br>3:30 | 1 | ↓ | ↓ | ↓ | ↓ | ↓ | | | | | | | | |
| | | | | | | | | | | | | | | |

Thursday

| | 3rd | | | 4th | | | 5th | | 6th | | | | | |
|---|---|---|---|---|---|---|---|---|---|---|---|---|---|---|
| | Bob | Bill | DAVE | RUTH | MATT | KIM | RICK | TARA | DON | TINA | | Ed | | |
| 9:10 9:30 | SHW | | SHW | B | R | SHW | R | ART | ART | ART | | MATH REG | | |
| 9:30 9:50 | PURPLE READ BOOK | | MHW | 5 | M | 3 | M | | | | | | | |
| 9:50 10:10 | R | LIBRARY | LIB | LIB. | | LIB | LIB | 10:00 | | | | ↓ | | |
| 10:10 10:30 | | | | | ↓ | | | SS | SS | SS | | L | | |
| 10:30 10:50 | | ↓ | 10:40 | ↓ | RHW | ↓ | ↓ | ↓ | ↓ | ↓ | | R | | |
| 10:50 11:10 | MHW | SEAT WORK R | R | READ INTER | MHW | RHW | RHW | RHW | RHW | RHW | | RHW | | |
| 11:10 11:30 | LION BOOK | RHW | 1 | | A | M | A | 3 | R | R | | 4 | | |
| 11:30 12:10 | 4 | SRA | M | ↓ | SHW | | MHW | SHW | RHW | 4 | | 1 | | |
| 12:10 1:10 | | | | L | U | N | C | H | | | | | | |
| 1:10 1:30 | ART | SS | SS | SS | SS | SS | SS | R | 1:15 MATH INTER | A | | A | | |
| 1:30 1:50 | | | | | | | | M | | M | | LIB | | |
| 1:50 2:10 | ↓ | L | L | L | L | L | 3 | A | | RED BOOK | | | | |
| 2:10 2:30 | [A] | SC | SC | SC | SC | SC | SC | SC | ↓ | ↓ | | 2:15 MATH | | |
| 2:30 2:50 | MATH INTER | | | | | | | | MATH BACK UP | MHW | | BACK UP SS | | |
| 2:50 3:10 | ↓ | A | 2:55 | A | L | A | L | LHW | 5 | SHW | | 3:00 | | |
| 3:10 3:30 | LHW | HOME WORK | HOME WORK | HOME WORK | HOME WORK | HOME WORK | HOME WORK | L | L | L | | HEALTH | | |
| | | | | | | | | | | | | 3:40 | | |

Friday

| | 3rd | | | 4th | | | 5th | | | 6th | | | | |
|---|---|---|---|---|---|---|---|---|---|---|---|---|---|---|
| | Bob | Bill | DAVE | RUTH | MATT | KIM | RICK | TARA | DON | TINA | | Ed | | |
| 9:10 9:30 | 1 | R | R | SS | R | LHW | SRA | SS | SS | SS | | 1 | | |
| 9:30 9:50 | R | RHW | RHW | ↓ | RHW | MISS G | 1 | ↓ | ↓ | ↓ | | SRA | | |
| 9:50 10:10 | S | | 1 | 4 | 4 | 5 | 5 | 10:20 | SEAT WORK | SEAT WORK | | BARNELL LOFT | | |
| 10:10 10:30 | RHW | MATH | MHW | MHW | 1 | 2 | LHW | S | R | R | | ART | | |
| 10:30 10:50 | MHW | ↓ | 5 | M | LHW | 4 | 6 | 1 | RHW | RHW | | ↓ | | |
| 10:50 11:10 | P.E. ↓ | LHW | LHW | MHW | MHW | R | R | RHW | 4 | 5 | | MATH INTEG | | |
| 11:10 11:30 | 11:25 | SS ↓ | SS ↓ | READ INTEG ↓ | SS ↓ | SS ↓ | SS ↓ | R | LHW | 1 | | | | |
| 11:30 12:10 | SHW | | | | | | | A | 3 | M | | 12:00 | | |
| 12:10 1:10 | | | | L | U | N | C | H | | | | | | |
| 1:10 1:30 | WRITING | SC ↓ | SC ↓ | SC ↓ | SC ↓ | SC ↓ | SC ↓ | S | S | S | | SS | | |
| 1:30 1:50 | 1:35 MATH INTEG ↓ | | | | | | | LIB ↓ | LIB. ↓ | LIB ↓ | | ↓ | | |
| 1:50 2:10 | | S | S | S | S | A | S | | | | | | | |
| 2:10 2:30 | | A | A | A | A | M | M | 2:15 SEAT WORK | | MHW | | R | | |
| 2:30 2:50 | MATH BACK UP | GYM ↓ | GYM ↓ | GYM ↓ | GYM ↓ | GYM ↓ | GYM ↓ | RHW | MATH INTEG ↓ | A | | L | | |
| 2:50 3:10 | A | | | | | | | MHW | | H | | 3:00 SCIENCE ↓ | | |
| 3:10 3:30 | DLM | 6 | M | 3 | M | KHW | MHW | HEALTH | | | | | | |
| | | | | | | | | | | | | 3:45 | | |

| | MONDAY | TUESDAY | WEDNESDAY | THURSDAY | FRIDAY |
|---|---|---|---|---|---|
| 1 | Planning Time or Audit Classes | Room 101<br>Joe - Math | Planning Time or Audit Classes | Room 101<br>Math<br>Joe | Room 101<br>Reading<br>Joe |
| 2 | Room - Bus. Room<br>Biology<br>Glenn | Room - Business Room<br>Math<br>Glenn | Room - Business Room<br>Lang. Arts<br>David<br>Glenn | Room - Business Rm.<br>Lang. Arts<br>David<br>Glenn | Room - Business Room<br>Biology<br>Glenn |
| 3 | Planning Time or Audit Classes | Planning Time or Audit Classes | Planning Time or Audit Classes | Planning Time or Audit Classes | Planning Time or Audit Classes |
| 4 | Planning Time or Audit Classes | Room 111<br>Lang. Arts<br>Joe | [Lunch] | Room 111<br>Lang. Arts<br>Joe | Planning Time or Audit Classes |
| 5 | Room 111<br>Reading<br>Barton<br>Dan Brad | Room 111<br>[Lunch] | Room 111<br>Reading<br>Dan Brad<br>Barton | Room 111<br>[Lunch] | Planning Time or Audit Classes |
| 6 | [Lunch] | Planning Time or Audit Classes | Planning Time or Audit Classes | Planning Time or Audit Classes | [Lunch] |
| 7 | Room 203<br>READING<br>David Barton<br>Glenn Brad<br>Joe Dan | Room 203<br>Lang Arts<br>Dan<br>Barton<br>Brad | Room 203<br>READING<br>David<br>Glenn<br>Joe | Room 203<br>Lang. Arts<br>David Brad<br>Dan Joe<br>Barton Glenn | Room 203<br>Lang. Arts<br>Dan Brad<br>Barton |
| 8 | Room 203<br>Math<br>David | Room 203<br>Reading<br>Dan Brad<br>Barton | Room 203<br>Math<br>David | Room 203<br>Math<br>David Barton<br>Dan Brad | Room 203<br>Math<br>David Brad<br>Dan<br>Barton |

| | Monday | Tuesday | Wednesday | Thursday | Friday |
|---|---|---|---|---|---|
| 1 | Ind. ARTS Bill / Phys Sci - C21 202 DON Bob Rick | — | IND ARTS - C21-61 Bill / Phys. Science - C21-202 DON BOB RICK | — | — |
| 2 | — | — | — | — | — |
| 3 | English - F37 107 Bill, Don BOB ⟷ | English 638-106 John ⟷ | English 108-86 DAVE ⟷ | Biology 104-F70 GEORGE ⟷ | ⟷ |
| 4 | Math 222 K48 DON, BOB Rick ⟷ | — | LUNCH | — | |
| 5 | — | LUNCH | — | LUNCH | Planning Time |
| 6 | LUNCH | GOVERN - 102 - C21 Bob, DAVE / ECON - 121 - C22 Rick, Bill | M. SURVEY - 116 - S72 GEORGE | Biology - 220 - C19 John | LUNCH |
| 7 | — | — | — | — | — |
| 8 | — | — | — | — | — |

# Learning Disabilities

| | M | T | W | Th | F |
|---|---|---|---|---|---|
| 1 Room | Nick R<br>Sheree S<br>Ricky R<br>323 | Nick R<br>Sheree S<br>Ricky R<br>323 | Nick R<br>Sheree S<br>Ricky R<br>Dani K<br>323 | Nick R<br>Sheree S<br>Ricky R<br>Dani K<br>323 | Nick R<br>Sheree S<br>Ricky R<br>323 |
| 2 Room | Nick R<br>Marcy W<br>Chuck K<br>Vince<br>323 | Marcy W<br>Chuck K<br>Johnny B<br>323 | Marcy W<br>Chuck K<br>Johnny B<br>Vince<br>323 | Marcy W<br>Chuck K<br>Johnny B<br>Vince<br>323 | Marcy W<br>Chuck K<br>Johnny B<br>Vince<br>323 |
| 3 | | Free | Period | | |
| 4 Room | Debby A<br>Eric K<br>Band Room | Debby A<br>Eric K<br>Band Room | Debby A<br>Eric K<br>Band Room | Debby A<br>Eric K<br>Band Room | Debby A<br>Eric K<br>Band R |
| 5 Room | Dani K<br>Laura<br>Bobby F<br>218 | Dani K<br>Laura<br>Bobby F<br>218 | Dani K<br>Laura<br>Bobby F<br>218 | Dani K<br>Laura<br>Bobby F<br>218 | Dani K<br>Laura<br>Bobby F<br>218 |
| 6 | Sheree S<br>Dave F | Sheree S<br>Dave F | Sheree S<br>Jimmy F | Sheree S<br>Jimmy F | Sheree S<br>Jimmy F |
| 7 Room | Valarie<br>218 | Valarie<br>218 | Valarie<br>218 | Valarie<br>218 | Valarie<br>218 |

WEEKLY GOALS

| Pupil | Monday | Tuesday | Wednesday | Thursday | Friday |
| --- | --- | --- | --- | --- | --- |
| | | | | | |
| | | | | | |
| | | | | | |
| | | | | | |
| | | | | | |
| | | | | | |
| | | | | | |

WEEKLY ACADEMIC PLAN ______________________________

| Reading | Math |
|---|---|
| Monday –<br>Tuesday –<br>Wednesday –<br>Thursday –<br>Friday –<br>Text –<br>Objectives – | Monday –<br>Tuesday –<br>Wednesday –<br>Thursday –<br>Friday –<br>Text –<br>Objectives – |
| **Phonics** | **Spelling** |
| Monday –<br>Tuesday –<br>Wednesday –<br>Thursday –<br>Friday –<br>Text –<br>Objectives – | Monday –<br>Tuesday –<br>Wednesday –<br>Thursday –<br>Friday –<br>Text –<br>Objectives – |
| **English** | |
| Monday –<br>Tuesday –<br>Wednesday –<br>Thursday –<br>Friday –<br>Text –<br>Objectives – | |

| Time | MONDAY | TUESDAY (time) | TUESDAY | WEDNESDAY (time) | WEDNESDAY | THURSDAY (time) | THURSDAY | FRIDAY (time) | FRIDAY |
|---|---|---|---|---|---|---|---|---|---|
| 8:15-8:45 | PLANNING TIME | | | | | | | | |
| 8:45-9:15 | READING | 8:45-10:00 | READING | 8:45-10:00 | MATH | 8:45-9:00<br>9:00-9:15 | SPELLING<br>READING | 8:45-9:00<br>9:00-9:15 | MATH<br>SPELLING |
| 9:15-9:30 | MATH | | | | | 9:15-9:45 | SPELLING | 9:15-9:45 | READING |
| 9:30-10:00 | READING | 10:00-10:30 | MATH | 10:00-11:45 | READING | 9:45-10:15 | READING | 9:45-10:00 | MATH |
| 10:00-10:45 | SPELLING | 10:30 10:45 | READING | | | 10:15-10:30<br>10:30-10:45 | MATH<br>SPELLING | 10:00-10:30 | SPELLING |
| 10:45-11:15 | READING | 10:45-11:00<br>11:00-11:30 | MATH<br>READING | | | 10:45-11:00<br>11:00-11:15 | READING<br>SPELLING | 10:30-11:00<br>11:00-11:30 | READING<br>MATH |
| 11:15-11:45 | MATH | 11:30-11:45 | LANGUAGE | | | 11:15-11:30<br>11:30-11:45 | MATH<br>SPELLING | 11:30-11:45 | READING |
| 11:45-12:15 | LUNCH | | | | | | | | |
| 12:15-1:00 | PLANNING TIME | | | | | | | | |
| 1:00-1:15 | READING | 1:00-1:30 | READING | 1:00-1:45 | READING | 1:00-1:15 | MATH | 1:00-1:15 | |
| 1:15-1:30 | SPELLING | | | | | 1:15-1:45 | READING | 1:15-1:30 | |
| 1:30-1:45 | READING | 1:30-1:45 | MATH | 1:45-2:00 | MATH | 1:45-2:00 | MATH | 1:30-1:45 | |
| 1:45-2:00 | SPELLING | 1:45-2:00 | MATH | 2:00-3:00 | READING | 2:00-2:30 | READING | 1:45-2:00 | |
| 2:00-2:15 | MATH | 2:00-3:00 | READING | | | 2:30-2:45 | MATH | 2:00-3:00 | INTEREST CLUBS |
| 2:15-2:30 | PLANNING | | | | | 2:45 | LANGUAGE | | |
| 2:30-2:45 | MATH | | | | | | | | |
| 3:00-3:45 | PLANNING TIME | | | | | | | | |

Monday — Master Schedule (4th + 5th grades)

| 8:30 - 9:00 | 10:00 - 10:20 | 11:00 - 11:30 | 12:55 - 1:15 | 1:55 - 2:15 | 2:55 - 3:15 |
|---|---|---|---|---|---|
| Planning Time<br>9:00 - 9:20<br>Bob - Health<br>Bill - Gym<br>Jeff - Math<br>Kim - Math<br>Pat #1<br>Larry #8<br>Rick - Gym<br>Mark - Gym | Bob Music<br>Bill Read Mr J.<br>Jeff S.S.<br>Kim #1<br>Pat Read Mr J.<br>Larry Music<br>Rick Seat Work<br>Mark Music | Bob S. Studies<br>Bill Math<br>Jeff Seat Work<br>Kim #5<br>Pat Seat Work<br>Larry Science<br>Rick Writing<br>Mark Science | Bob Seat Work<br>Bill Seat Work<br>Jeff #2<br>Kim Art<br>Larry Math } Mr K.<br>Rick Math }<br>Mark #3 | Bob Lang<br>Bill Lang<br>Jeff Soc Studies<br>Kim #5<br>Larry Lang<br>Rick Art<br>Mark Speech | Bob Art<br>Bill Soc Studies<br>Jeff Science<br>Kim Math<br>Larry Soc Studies<br>Rick Soc Studies<br>Mark Science |
| **9:20 - 9:40** | **10:20 - 10:40** | **11:30 - 12:15** | **1:15 - 1:35** | **2:15 - 2:35** | **3:15 - 3:40** |
| Bob #8<br>Bill Read<br>Jeff Gym<br>Kim Math<br>Pat Math<br>Larry #7<br>Rick #1<br>Mark #2 | Bob Soc Studies<br>Bill Music<br>Jeff Seat Work<br>Kim #4<br>Larry #2<br>Rick Gym<br>Mark Reading | Lunch & Preparation<br>12:15 - 12:35<br>Bob Sci<br>Bill Lunch<br>Jeff #8<br>Kim Math - Mrs K<br>Larry #1<br>Rick Lunch<br>Mark Math | Bob - Math<br>Bill Seat Work<br>Jeff Math<br>Kim Music<br>Larry Art<br>Rick #2<br>Mark Soc Studies | Bob Seat Work<br>Bill Soc Studies<br>Jeff Soc Studies<br>Kim Science<br>Larry Soc Studies<br>Rick Math<br>Mark Speech | Bob Art<br>Bill Sci<br>Jeff Health<br>Kim #2<br>Larry Seat Work<br>Rick Soc Studies<br>Mark Science |
| **9:40 - 10:00** | **10:40 - 11:00** | **12:35 - 12:55** | **1:35 - 1:55** | **2:35 - 2:55** | |
| Bob Seat Work<br>Bill Seat Work<br>Jeff Seat Work<br>Kim Read } Mrs J.<br>Pat Read }<br>Larry Writing<br>Rick #2<br>Mark #8 | Bob Soc Studies<br>Bill Seat Work<br>Jeff #4<br>Kim Seat Work<br>Larry #7<br>Rick Read Mr. X<br>Mark #5 | Bob - Sci<br>Bill Lunch<br>Jeff Seat Work<br>Kim Art<br>Larry Lunch<br>Rick } Lunch<br>Mark } | Bob - Read<br>Bill #2<br>Jeff Seat Work<br>Kim Music<br>Larry #1<br>Rick Soc Studies<br>Mark - Math | Bob Art<br>Bill Soc Studies<br>Jeff Sci<br>Kim Soc Studies<br>Larry Science<br>Rick - Read<br>Mark - Read | |

# Student's Weekly Schedules

Most special education teachers who use schedules make one schedule a week. Pages 119-122 are sample schedules from an LD room.

The vertical axis contains time segments, and the horizontal axis contains the days of the week. It should be noted that direct instruction is indicated by the teacher or aide as simply Mrs. J. or Mrs. B.

The various numbers match the learning centers that are assigned. The learning centers must be changed often when they are used as permanent assignments. Some teachers laminate these student schedules and alter the center assignment with a water-based felt tip marker. This particular teacher color codes corresponding centers and numbers (check teacher's notes about active child on 121).

Page 123 depicts a schedule for an older student. It should be noted that periods are longer. More attention and more production is expected.

Page 124 is not only crossways instead of lengthwise, but, in fact, represents a blank page for the teacher. The area filled in represents the time the student is out of the room and marked in red (color not shown in this book). Therefore, the teacher has only to fill in the empty blocks weekly for a completed intermediate student's schedule.

Page 125 depicts an original schedule made and used by an aide. Based on the IEP, there are certain activities and curricula prescribed and typed which are evaluated by the aide.

Page 126 represents another original tool rather than a schedule per se. This format is for a student with more independence. Time blocks are not used, but the assignments are jotted in for student guidance. The teacher might also use this to write in time blocks for direct instruction.

| | TIME | MONDAY | TUESDAY | WEDNESDAY | THURSDAY | FRIDAY |
|---|---|---|---|---|---|---|
| 1 | 9:00 | Mrs. J. | | Mrs. J. | Mrs. J. | Mrs. J. |
| 2 | 9:15 | Mrs. B. | | One too many | Workbook → | |
| 3 | 9:30 | Workbook | Gym | 1 ③ | | |
| 4 | 9:45 | | | 10 | | |
| 5 | 10:00 | | Music | 10 | | |
| 6 | 10:15 | | | 3 | | |
| 7 | 10:30 | Mrs. J. | | Mrs. J. | Mrs. J. | Mrs. J. |
| 8 | 10:45 | 2 | 2 | 2 | 2 | |
| 9 | 11:00 | 14 | 1 ② | 14 | 1 | |
| 10 | 11:15 | Mrs. B. | Mrs. B. | Mrs. B. | Mrs. B. | IMC |
| 11 | 11:30 | 5 | 4-B | 4-C | 4-D | |
| 12 | 11:45 | 5 | 6 | 6 | 6 | |
| 13 | 12:00 | | | | | |
| 14 | 12:15 | | Lunch | | | |
| 15 | 12:30 | Records | Mrs. B. | Puzzles | | Library |
| 16 | 12:45 | Mrs. J. | Mrs. J. | Mrs. J. | | Mrs. J. |
| 17 | 1:00 | 16 + Diary | 16 + Diary | 16 + Diary | Swim | |
| 18 | 1:15 | | | | | |
| 19 | 1:30 | S | C I | E N | C E | |
| 20 | 1:45 | | | | Art | |
| 21 | 2:00 | | 14 | Pegboard | 14 | |
| 22 | 2:15 | 1 ① | 13 | 13 | 13 | |
| 23 | 2:30 | Mrs. B. | Mrs. B. | Mrs. B. | Mrs. B. | Mrs. B. |
| | | | | | | |

| | TIME | MONDAY | TUESDAY | WEDNESDAY | THURSDAY | FRIDAY |
|---|---|---|---|---|---|---|
| 1 | 9:00 | Mrs. T. | Hearing & Lang. | Mrs. T. | Mrs. T. | |
| 2 | 9:15 | 6 | Mrs. A. | | Records | |
| 3 | 9:30 | Puzzles | Pegboard | Speech & Lang. | | Gym |
| 4 | 9:45 | Mrs. A. | 1 (1) | Mrs. A. | | Swim & Music |
| 5 | 10:00 | | 1 (2) | Mrs. R. | 1 (3) | |
| 6 | 10:15 | 2 | 2 | 2 | 2 | |
| 7 | 10:30 | 3 | | 3 | | |
| 8 | 10:45 | 4-A | Swim | Pegboard | | One too many |
| 9 | 11:00 | Workbook | Gym | One too many | Art | 1 (4) |
| 10 | 11:15 | 7 | | | | 2 |
| 11 | 11:30 | | Lunch | | | |
| 12 | 11:45 | | | | | |
| 13 | 12:00 | 16 | 14 | 16 | 16 | 16 |
| 14 | 12:15 | 14 | Mrs. R. | 14 | 14 | 14 |
| 15 | 12:30 | Mrs. T. | 13 | Mrs. T. | Mrs. T. | Mrs. T. |
| 16 | 12:45 | 9 | 3 | 8 | | Pegboard |
| 17 | 1:00 | 13 | Records | 8 | 3 | Records |
| 18 | 1:15 | Mrs. R. | Mrs. R. | Mrs. R. | Mrs. R. | Mrs. R. |
| 19 | 1:30 | 10 | Puzzle | 13 | 13 | 13 |
| 20 | 1:45 | 10 | 4-B | 6 | Puzzles | Mrs. A. |
| 21 | 2:00 | | 6 | 4-C | 6 | IMC |
| 22 | 2:15 | Miss Fr. | Mrs. T. | 11 | Workbook | Mrs. T. |
| 23 | 2:30 | Mrs. R. | Mrs. R. | Mrs. R. | Mrs. R. | Mrs. R. |
| | | | | | | |

| | TIME | MONDAY | TUESDAY | WEDNESDAY | THURSDAY | FRIDAY |
|---|---|---|---|---|---|---|
| 1 | 9:00 | Mrs. P. | Mrs. P. | Mrs. P. | Mrs. P. | Mrs. P. |
| 2 | 9:15 | | | Mrs. P. | IMC | |
| 3 | 9:30 | Mrs. P. | Mrs. C. | Mrs. C. | Mrs. P. | Mrs. P. |
| 4 | 9:45 | | | Pegboard | Pegboard | Pegboard |
| 5 | 10:00 | Pegboard | Pegboard | | Speech | Miscue |
| 6 | 10:15 | Mrs. P. | Mrs. P. | Mrs. P. | Mrs. P. | Mrs. P. |
| 7 | 10:30 10:35 | ART | | | Math | |
| 8 | 10:45 | | 3 | Swim & Gym | 3 | 7 |
| 9 | 11:00 | | Mrs. P. | | Workbook | Record |
| 10 | 11:15 11:20 | | | | | |
| 11 | 11:30 | Lunch | | | | |
| 12 | 11:45 | | | | | |
| 13 | 12:00 | 1 ① | 1 ② | 1 ③ | 1 ④ | 16 |
| 14 | 12:15 | 2 | 2 | 2 | 2 | 2 |
| 15 | 12:30 | 16 | Library | | Mrs. C. | Puzzles |
| 16 | 12:45 | 13 | 13 | 13 | 13 | Music |
| 17 | 1:00 | 6 | 6 | 6 | Mrs. C. | |
| 18 | 1:15 | 3 | Puzzles | 3 | 6 | |
| 19 | 1:30 | Workbook | Records | 8 | Puzzles | Swim & Gym |
| 20 | 1:45 | Puzzles | 9 | 8 | 10 | |
| 21 | 2:00 | 4A | 11 | 11 | 10 | 13 |
| 22 | 2:15 | | 16 | | | Jean reads to you |
| 23 | 2:30 | Mrs. P. | Mrs. P. | Mrs. P. | Mrs. P. | Mrs. P. |
| | | | | | | |

2nd grade - very active - must be kept busy at all times.

| | TIME | MONDAY | TUESDAY | WEDNESDAY | THURSDAY | FRIDAY |
|---|---|---|---|---|---|---|
| 1 | 9:00 | Mrs. S. | Swim & Gym<br>Art | Mrs. S. | Mrs. S. | Mrs. S. |
| 2 | 9:15 | 2 | | 2 | 2 | 2 |
| 3 | 9:30 | Workbook | | 15 | Workbook | One too many |
| 4 | 9:45 | 3 | | Think & Do | 5 | 6 |
| 5 | 10:00 | 7 | | Jack & Julie | 16 & Diary | 8 |
| 6 | 10:15 | 15 | | 4-C | 4-D | 8 |
| 7 | 10:30 | 12 | | 14 & 16 | 14 | 14 & 16 |
| 8 | 10:45 | Mrs. K. | Mrs. K. | Mrs. K. | Mrs. K. | Mrs. K. |
| 9 | 11:00 | Mrs. S. | Mrs. S. | Mrs. S. | Mrs. S. | 10 |
| 10 | 11:15 | Diary & Record | Diary & Record | Diary & Record | 9 | 10 |
| 11 | 11:30 | | Math | | | |
| 12 | 11:45 | | | | | |
| 13 | 12:00 | | Lunch | | | |
| 14 | 12:15 | | | | | |
| 15 | 12:30 | | | | | |
| 16 | 12:45 | | | | Swim & Gym<br>Music | |
| 17 | 1:00 | Social Studies & Science | | | | |
| 18 | 1:15 | | | | | |
| 19 | 1:30 | | | | | |
| 20 | 1:45 | | | | | |
| 21 | 2:00 | 13 | Think & Do | 3 | Jack & Julie | Mrs. S. |
| 22 | 2:15 | 13 | 1 ① | 1 ② | 1 ③ | Puzzle |
| 23 | 2:30 | Mrs. K. | Mrs. K. | Mrs. K. | Mrs. K. | Mrs. K. |
| | | | | | | |

| | | | | | |
|---|---|---|---|---|---|
| 9:10 - 9:30 | Writing | Reading | Reading | music | Gym |
| 9:30 - 9:50 | Gym 9:45 | | | | |
| 9:50 - 10:10 | | | | Mrs. S | Reading |
| 10:10 - 10:30 | Recess | MHW | 3 | Reading | |
| 10:30 - 10:50 | Reading | Science | Science | | |
| 10:50 - 11:10 | | | | | Science |
| 11:10 - 11:30 | | writing | 5 | Math | |
| 11:30 - 11:50 | L | U | N | C | H |
| 11:50 - 12:10 | | | | | |
| 12:10 - 12:30 | | | | | |
| 12:30 - 12:50 | | | | | |
| 12:50 - 1:10 | Math | Math | 4 1:05 | 2 | MHW |
| 1:10 - 1:30 | Social Studies | MHW | Art | 1 | SRA |
| 1:30 - 1:50 | | Health | | Language | Math |
| 1:50 - 2:10 | 2:00 Seatwork | Social Studies | Spelling | LHW | Social Studies |
| 2:10 - 2:30 | Science | | 1 | Barnell Loft 2:20 Social Studies | |
| 2:30 - 2:50 | | | Math 2:45 | | writing |
| 2:50 - 3:10 | 6 3:00 | Language | Library | | 3:00 Math Push |
| 3:10 - 3:30 | Spelling | LHW | | writing | Spelling |
| | Take Spelling Home | | Take math Home | | Take math Home |

| | Monday | Tuesday | Wednesday | Thursday | Friday |
|---|---|---|---|---|---|
| 9 – 9:15 | Aide | Aide | Aide | Aide | Aide |
| 9:15 – 9:30 | | | | | |
| 9:30 – 9:45 | | | | | |
| 9:45 – 10 | | | | | SPEECH |
| 10 – 10:15 | | | | | |
| 10:15 – 10:30 | | | | | |
| 10:30 – 10:45 | Reading | Math / SPell. | Reading | Math / Re-test SPELL. | Reading / Final test |
| 10:45 – 11:10 | Gym | Art | GYM | Art | Music |
| 11:10 – 11:30 | | | | | |
| 11:30 – 11:50 | | | | | |
| 1 – 1:15 | | | | | |
| 1:15 – 1:30 | | | | | |
| 1:30 – 1:45 | | | | | |
| 1:45 – 2 | Math | Math | Math | Math | Math |
| 2 – 2:30 | | | | | |
| | | | | | |

WEDNESDAY

DATE: 1/7/82

| 9:05 SPELLING | 9:25 SPELLING | 9:45 CURSIVE | 10:05 SPELLING |
|---|---|---|---|
| Follett Sp. Patterns<br>Page 69 Book B<br>Ricky 100% Pre-test<br>Eric 100%<br>Tara 100%<br>John 100% ✓<br>Billy 100%<br>Check work in Sp. books | Pretest<br>Sheree 100%<br>Kim 100%<br>Lesson #9 Page ___<br>CVC short u ✓ | Sheree<br>Kim ★<br>Tara ★<br>✓<br>Vanguard<br>#4 review c | Basic Goals in Sp.<br>Level 6 L 9 Page 21<br>Pretest ✓<br>Dan absent<br>Marcy 100% |
| **10:25 DAILY NEWS** | **10:45 MONEY** | **11:05 SOCIAL STUDIES** | **11:25 MARCY** |
| Children dictate news as I write it on the board Billy reads, and points; then calls on other students to read.<br>Debby ★ Eric ★<br>Sheree ★ Ricky ★<br>Kim ★ Billy ★ | Money Makes Sense<br>Page 27 (Sp.<br>Debby Kim ★<br>Sheree skipped<br>and running late<br>*Kim - Lunch 11:00) | Regions & Social Needs<br>Review Pages 123-125<br>Eric ✓ So. Am<br>Vince ✓ Rain Forest<br>John ✓ | Homeroom<br>Clerical |
| **11:45 WRITING** | **12:05 LUNCH** | **12:25 LUNCH** | **12:50 S. O. S.** |
| Debby ___<br>Review Aa-Bb-<br>absent<br>Introduce Cc Dd | ✓ | ✓ | Sound Level 1<br>Order Book 1<br>Sense Page 43-45<br>Debby absent<br>Sheree ★ ★<br>Kim ★ 9<br>Tara ★ ★ |
| **1:10 TIME** | **1:30 A. D. D.** | **1:50** | **2:10 PHONICS** |
| Working on Quarter-Past<br>Sheree absent<br>Kim ★<br>Debby - Music 1:15 absent ✓ | Tara<br>Ricky<br>Billy<br>Review short vowels<br>Introduce ..........<br>sh ch | ✓<br>Clerical<br>Trace + Cut Butterflies for bulletin board | Debby absent<br>Sheree ending<br>Kim ★ sounds<br>Boardwork<br>dictated words<br>CVC pattern |
| **2:30 ~~MATH~~ Money** | **2:50** | **3:10 DISMISSAL** | **COMMENTS:** |
| Reinforce Time ↔<br>Vince Homeroom<br>John | Took down old bulletin board<br>Butterflies for seatwork | | Electric off for an hour AM |

| | | | | |
|---|---|---|---|---|
| | | | | |
| MONDAY | TUESDAY | WEDNESDAY | THURSDAY | FRIDAY |
| | | | | |
| | | | | |
| | | | | |
| | | | | |
| | | | | |
| | | | | |
| | | | | |
| | | | | |
| MONDAY | TUESDAY | WEDNESDAY | THURSDAY | FRIDAY |

# Student's Daily Schedules

This section provides samples of individual daily schedules used with primary daily schedules. The drawback with this type of schedule is the extensive time involved in completing them each day. However, they are effective in teaching structure and creating a climate for the internalization of time. They are, indeed, individualization at its best.

Page 130 demonstrates an open-ended style in which the time is filled in on the right hand vertical axis while the event remains stable. Illustrations assist students in identifying the activity, so reading isn't a prerequisite.

Pages 131-132 use clocks in a similar schedule. Page 131 is limited to four numbers and activities and represents the most basic type of scheduling. Page 132 has a similar cartoon format.

Page 133 represents a daily schedule without clocks or cartoons and is, therefore, usable with older students on a daily basis.

NAME DATE

Reading Mrs. Cooper

Math 1 2 3 4 5 6 7

Seatwork

Tracking

Phono or tape

Writing a b c d e f

Game

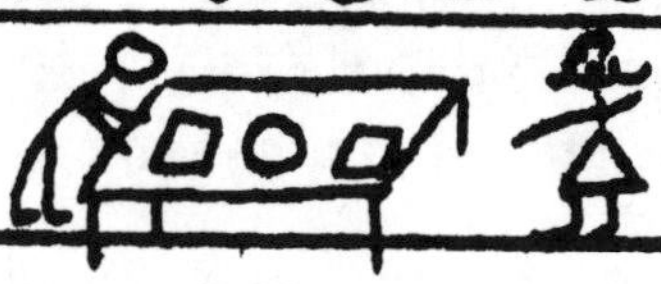

Visual Work Mrs. Konefal

Mrs. Cooper

Patterns

Auditory Work - Mrs. Konefal

Name
1.
Reading
2.
Mrs. Jones
3.
Seatwork
4.
Tape Recorder

| TIME | PERIOD | DAY NAME |
|---|---|---|
| | | |
| 9:00 | 1 | Seatwork |
| 9:15 | 2 | Reading |
| 9:30 | 3 | Tape Recorder |
| 9:45 | 4 | $\begin{array}{r}2\\+2\\\hline\end{array}$ Math |
| 10:00 | 5 | Record Player |
| 10:15 | 6 | Recess |
| 10:30 | 7 | Special: Art, Gym, Music |
| 10:45 | 8 | Seatwork |
| 11:00 | 9 | Lunch |

Group A

Name ______________________________

9:00 Reading

9:20 Seatwork

9:40 Spelling

10:10 Recess

# Bibliography

Doll, E.A. 1965. *Vineland social maturity scale.* Circle Pines, MN: American Guidance Service.

Arena, J. 1989. *How to write an IEP.* Novato, CA: Academic Therapy Publications.

Ayres, A.J. 1952. *The Ayres space test.* Los Angeles: Western Psychological Services.

Ayres, A.J. 1969. *Southern California perceptual motor tests.* Los Angeles: Western Psychological Services.

Baker, H.J. and L.B. 1967. *Detroit tests of learning aptitude.* Austin, TX: Pro-Ed Publishers.

Barbe, W. 1975. *Barbe reading skills.* West Nyack, NY: Center for Applied Research in Education.

Brigance, A.H. 1976. *The Brigance diagnostic inventory of basic skills.* Woburn, MA: Curriculum Associates.

Carrow, E. 1974. *Carrow elicited language inventory.* Austin, TX: Learning Concepts.

Kirk, S. & Kirk, W. 1971. *Illinois test of psycholinguistic abilities, revised.* Urbana, IL: University of Illinois Press.

Lindamood, C.H. and Lindamood, P.C. 1971. *Lindamood auditory conceptualization test.* Boston: Teaching Resources.

Markoff, A.M. 1992. *Within reach: Academic achievement through parent-teacher communication.* Novato, CA: Academic Therapy Publications.

Miller, W.H. 1978. *Reading diagnosis kit.* Center for Applied Research in Education, Inc. West Nyack, NY.

Gray, W.S. 1967. *Gray oral reading test.* Austin, TX: Pro-Ed Publishers.

Reid, D.K. 1988. *Teaching the learning disabled.* New York: Allyn and Bacon, Inc.

Rosner, J. 1975. *Helping children overcome learning difficulties.* New York: Walker and Company.

Science Research Associates. n.d. *Diagnosis reading/mathematics.* Chicago, IL.

Shinsky, E.J. *Techniques for including students with disabilities.* Shinsky Seminars, 3101 N. Cambridge Road, Lansing, MI.

Suiter, M. 1974. *Teacher's handbook of diagnostic screening: Auditory, motor, visual, language.* New York: Allyn and Bacon.

Wepman, J. 1973. *Wepman test of auditory discrimination.* New York: Language Research Associates.

# About the Authors

**Beverly School, PhD,** works with 42 school districts in her capacity as administrative supervisor of the Learning Support and Pre-School Programs in the Allegheny Intermediate Unit, Pittsburgh, Pennsylvania. She has taught elementary, secondary and handicapped children in Pennsylvania and California. Dr. School has been an adjunct professor in the Graduate Education Department at Duquesne University. She is contracted by the Right to Education Office, Harrisburg, Pennsylvania, to conduct due process hearings for special education.

In 1990, she served as president of the Three Rivers Chapter of Phi Delta Kappa. She has spent 33 years as a professional in the field of education, teaching regular education as well as special education students.

**Arlene Cooper, PhD,** had been a teacher of learning disabled students prior to becoming an instructional advisor for the school districts within the Allegheny Intermediate Unit in the Pittsburgh area, and is now retired. Dr. Cooper also served on the board of Allegheny County Association for Learning Disabilities.

# STORIES ON STONE

ROCK ART: IMAGES FROM THE ANCIENT ONES

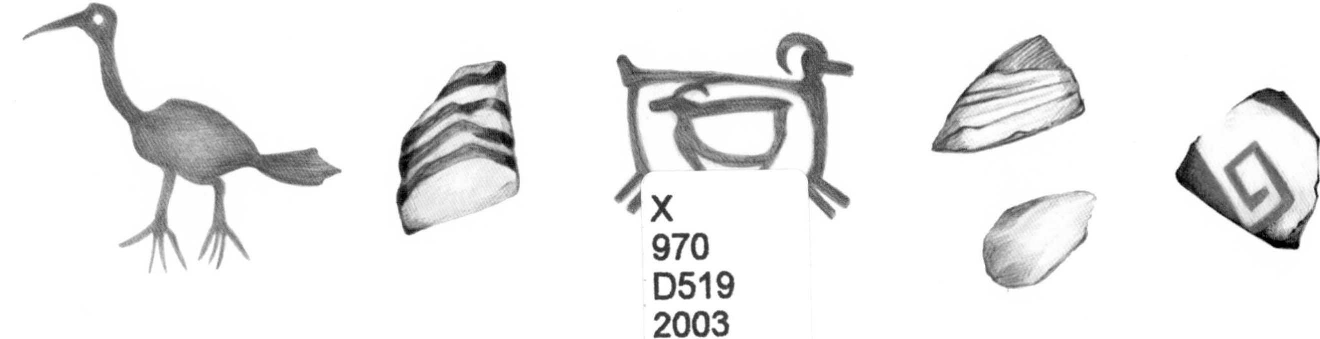



Jennifer Owings Dewey

University of New Mexico Press
Albuquerque

**In Memory of the Anasazi**

AND

**To the Memory of Bud Whiteford, with gratitude for his assistance and enthusiastic support**



Originally published in 1996 by Little, Brown & Company, ISBN 0-316-18211-7.
University of New Mexico Press edition published 2003 by arrangement with the author.

Library of Congress Cataloging-in-Publication Data

Dewey, Jennifer.
Stories on stone : rock art : images from the ancient ones /
Jennifer Owings Dewey.
p. cm.
Originally published: Boston : Little, Brown, 1996.
Summary: Text and illustrations introduce the rock art of the American Southwest, describing how the images were created and some of the likely inspirations behind them.
ISBN 0-8263-3024-X (cloth : alk. paper)
1. Pueblo Indians—Antiquities—Juvenile literature.
2. Petroglyphs—Southwest, New—Juvenile literature.
3. Rock paintings—Southwest, New—Juvenile literature.
4. Indians of North America—Southwest, New—Antiquities—Juvenile literature.
5. Southwest, New—Antiquities—Juvenile literature. [1. Pueblo Indians—Antiquities.
2. Rock paintings. 3. Indians of North America—Southwest, New—Antiquities.
4. Southwest, New—Antiquities.]
I. Title.
E99.P9 D38 2003
979'.01—dc22

2003011954

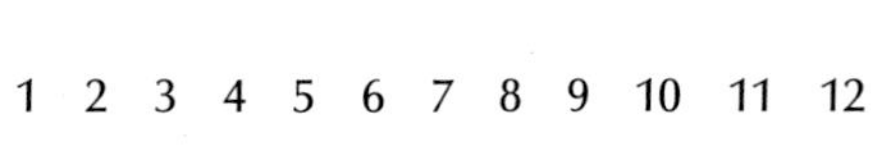

1 2 3 4 5 6 7 8 9 10 11 12

# Contents

# The People, Who Were They?

When I was a child, growing up in the Southwest, my family took car trips. We often went in search of rock art — ancient images on stone that are found throughout the region.

One hot July day, my parents, brother, and I walked single file along a ridge in the Mimbres Valley, a rock art site in southern New Mexico. The stone under our feet was volcanic — black boulders tumbled on a steep slope. Pecked into the rock surfaces were hundreds, if not thousands, of images. There were pictures of birds, snakes, deer, mountain sheep, and suns.

Some of the figures were eight feet tall. Others were six feet high, or three. Some measured only inches. To my eyes, each one was magical and strange.

A picture of a turtle caught my eye. I tried to imagine the person who had created it. I had been reading and studying all I could about rock art. And although little is known of the people who chipped out the rock images in the Mimbres Valley, since they left few traces of their lives behind, I knew enough to help my imagination along.

I knew that the turtle's creator might have lived in the valley two thousand years before my visit there. I decided the artist was a man — thin, with long black hair hanging loose. I pictured him pecking at the black volcanic rock with a hard stone, one he had used again and again.

I imagined the man was a husband and father, with a wife and children waiting for him in a grove of cottonwoods not far off. There, too, would be the other members of his clan. Many clans — bands of people who lived and traveled together — took their names from animals. Perhaps this clan had named itself after the turtle.

I imagined that the man was making the turtle to thank the spirits for good luck in hunting — or perhaps to ask for better luck in the next hunt.

Once finished with his work, the man would rejoin his family and clan members in the trees. He would know that anyone passing would see the turtle and understand what it meant.

On another family trip, we visited Nine Mile Canyon, a remote rock art site in southern Utah. We hiked deep into the canyon, where I saw images painted on sandstone walls. Some of the pictures were of kachinas, spirits that are half human, half god. The kachina figures were ten feet tall, with boxy bodies and shields. Their faces were covered by masks decorated with zigzags and circles.

I also saw painted images of antelope, bird tracks, and mountain sheep, as well as handprints — many of which fit my own ten-year-old hands. Later I learned that handprints are universal. They exist on walls and stone all around the world.

Rock art occurs wherever people once lived or camped. These marks on stone say, "We were here. We traveled this way." These pictures are a mysterious but readable record of human history.

Before the advent of written language, people lived as nomads. They traveled in small bands and tribes, following seasonal cycles. They wintered in caves and summered in temporary camps. To eat, they hunted, trapped small game, and gathered wild food.

Until the end of the last Ice Age, no humans yet roamed the wilderness of what is now North America. But when the ice receded, it exposed a land bridge from northern Asia to North America, and bands of nomads migrated across it. They were the true discoverers of America.

Small scattered bands trekked across forested plains and grassy prairies, making their way toward warmer climates than those they had left behind. Some found the southwestern region of the continent to their liking, and so they remained.

There were many tribes in the region, and each had its own language. In the beginning, these people, now called paleo-Indians, kept their nomadic way of life. Some of their descendants live as nomads today. But then an important discovery made its way north from Mexico: the art of farming. Not all tribes took up this new lifeway, but most did. They continued to hunt and trap as well, but now they no longer had to wander in search of food and shelter. They could become settled.

No one knows just when it happened, that discovery of saving seeds and planting them in the ground. We do know that early southwestern people planted corn, squash, and beans. They invented systems of ditches to carry scarce rainwater to their crops. When fields were harvested, the food was stored in stone granaries to keep it safe from rodents.

Farming tribes gathered in settlements on mesa tops and in river valleys. They built permanent dwellings — well-constructed pueblos, or towns — out of stone.

One of the most important cultures of the ancient Southwest was the Anasazi. The name means "ancient ones" or perhaps "enemies of ancient ones." No one agrees on the true meaning. Made up of many tribes, the Anasazi culture emerged about two thousand years ago.

The Anasazi were not alone in choosing a village way of life. Nor were they the first. However, they grew to be the most populous and widely dispersed of the early people who settled in the high desert and mountainous areas of the region.

Traces of the Anasazi exist all across their ancestral homelands. We can still see remains of cliff houses; kivas, or sacred rooms; granaries; and rock art.

To fathom the Anasazi, one must read the signs they left behind — their stories on stone.

# Myths, Spirits, and Shooting Stars

When I was very young and just beginning my quest for knowledge of rock art, a friend of my parents, a woman artist, agreed to let me tag along on trips she took to Anasazi sites.

One day, we hiked along the edge of the Rio Grande, New Mexico's longest and biggest river. There are many rock art sites along the river, on both the east and west banks.

On that day, the two of us scrambled and crawled over huge boulders of black volcanic rock. Most of the rock surfaces had images pecked out of them.

There were stick figures, such as a child might draw. There were lizards with long claws, turkey tracks, and roadrunners with their long tails up. There were faces with bulging eyes and snakes in coils. Some of the images looked like dancers.

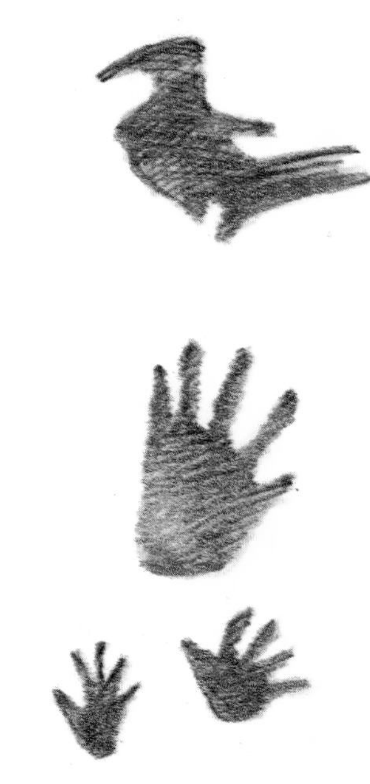

I was so taken with what I saw, I decided to do rock art myself. Perhaps Anasazi children had pecked pictures on stone. Why not me? I experimented and soon learned it is more difficult to make rock art than it appears.

To create images on stone, the Anasazi used resources they discovered in the landscape around them.

The word for a pecked or chipped image is *petroglyph.* The tool used to create petroglyphs is usually flint, a common kind of stone in the Southwest.

Painted images are called pictographs. To create them, the ancient ones made brushes out of yucca fibers, twigs, and animal hairs. They tied these into bundles with string made from animal gut cut into strips.

Paints were made by mixing animal blood, fat, or the whites of wild bird eggs with crushed flowers, plant roots, or minerals. Black came from charcoal or roasted graphite. Other colors were made by grinding down copper ore, which gave blues and greens, or iron oxide for reds.

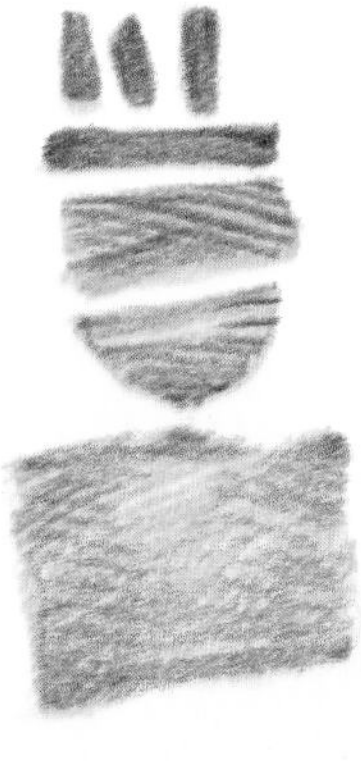

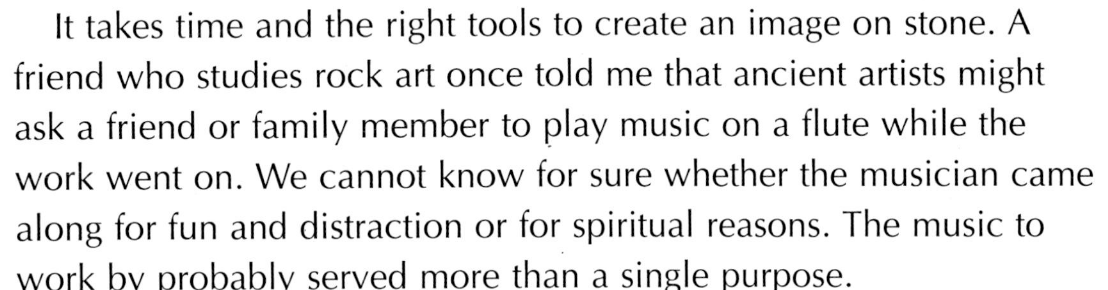

It takes time and the right tools to create an image on stone. A friend who studies rock art once told me that ancient artists might ask a friend or family member to play music on a flute while the work went on. We cannot know for sure whether the musician came along for fun and distraction or for spiritual reasons. The music to work by probably served more than a single purpose.

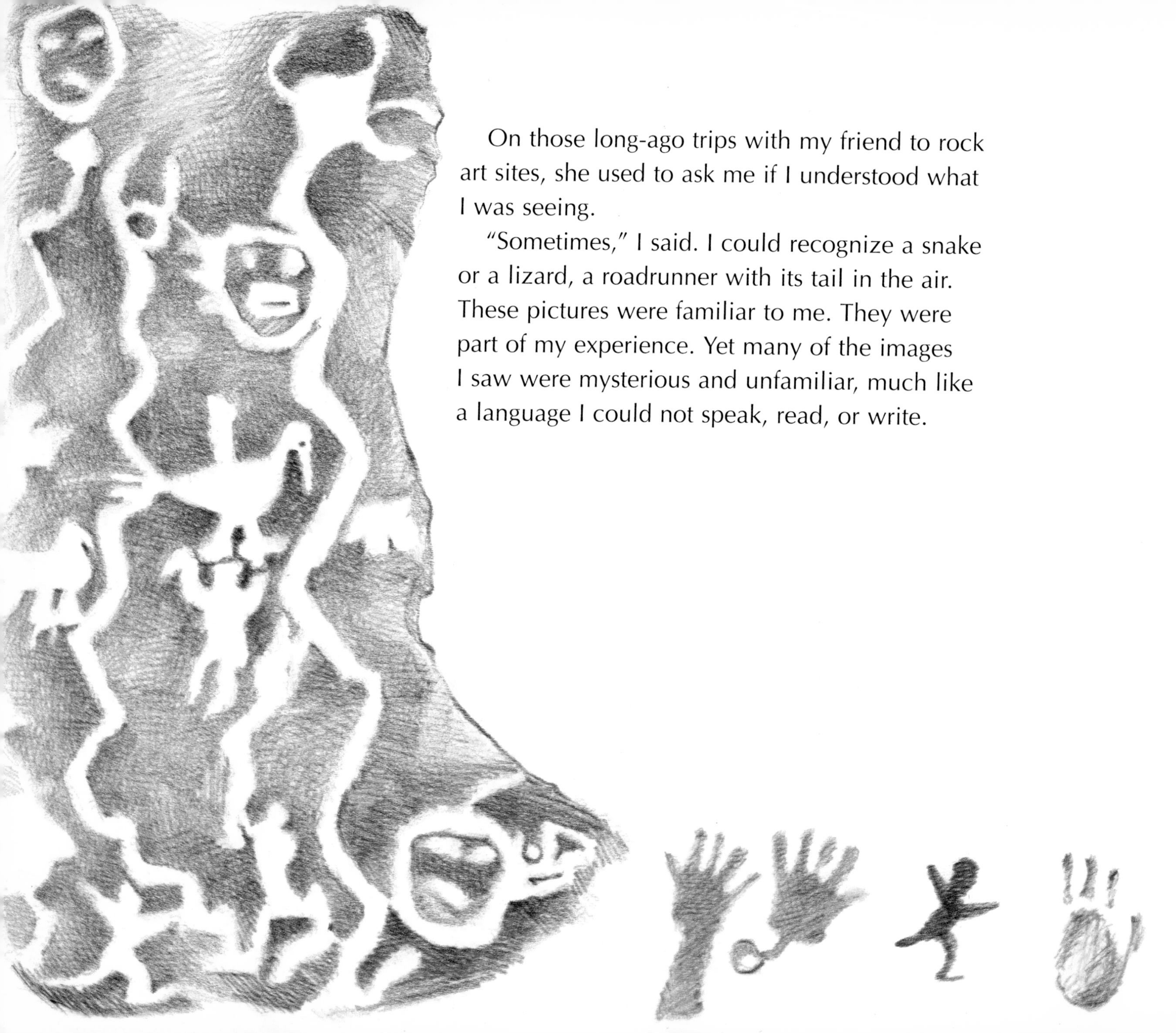

On those long-ago trips with my friend to rock art sites, she used to ask me if I understood what I was seeing.

"Sometimes," I said. I could recognize a snake or a lizard, a roadrunner with its tail in the air. These pictures were familiar to me. They were part of my experience. Yet many of the images I saw were mysterious and unfamiliar, much like a language I could not speak, read, or write.

One day, we saw an image of a mask with a long nose. "Do you know what that is?" she asked me. I did not know then and still have no certain answer.

A creature as common as a lizard becomes a different animal once it comes to exist on a rock surface. The meaning of the image was certainly wider and deeper for the maker than for me, a modern person.

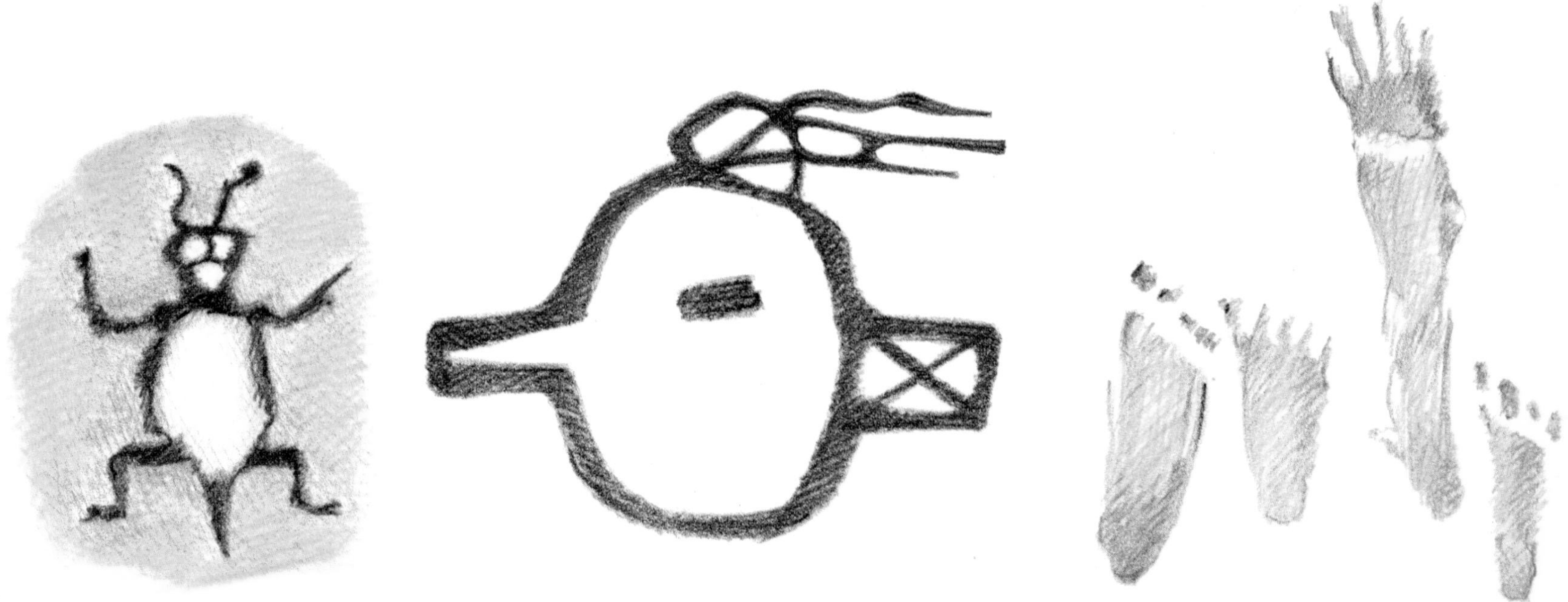

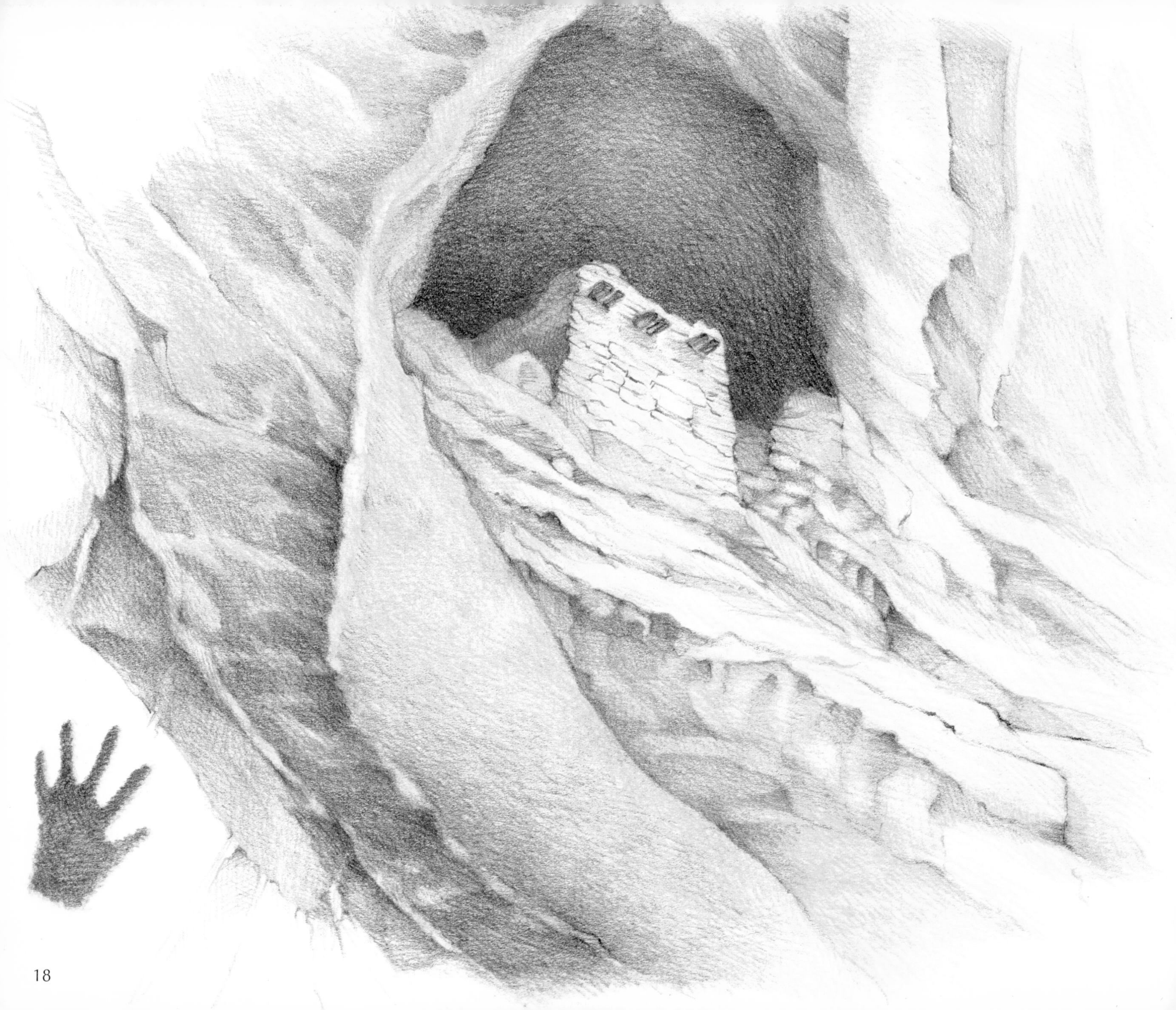

When I was still new to learning about rock art, my artist friend took me to a place where stone houses had been built on a ledge in a canyon wall. Narrow paths led to the dwellings, one hundred feet or more above the canyon floor.

The paths were so old that they cut ruts into the rock. As we climbed, I found a tiny turquoise bead and many bits of broken pottery. Then I saw a drawing of a humpbacked flute player.

"What is that?" I asked.

"Kokopelli," she told me. "A magic man, a spirit being. To some, because he has a bent back, he is especially wise. To others, he is a trickster — someone who makes mischief."

I puzzled over what she said to me. In my culture, someone with a bent back was not considered wise or special.

Since that time, I have come to know that Kokopelli means different things to different people at various times. Though his true meaning may remain unrevealed, I knew when I saw him that he had magic powers, if not for me directly then for somebody sometime.

Since we are not them, the Anasazi, we can only imagine what they felt as they pecked or painted their stories on stone.

Those who study rock art and attempt to translate the past say that many different sorts of people created pictographs and petroglyphs. Among them were medicine men and women, who possessed holy powers. These people were able to bridge the gap between the world of spirits and that of everyday. They made many of the images we see today.

Other, less holy, more ordinary people were given the task of recording the daily life of the pueblo, or town. Sometimes these people made pictures on stones to describe the birth of a new baby, the death of a parent, or the arrival of a swarm of insects. They also made images of celestial events, such as a solar eclipse or a meteor shower.

When I was twelve, I came upon the image of a shooting star chipped into the surface of a darkly colored rock. The picture was small, less than a foot across. People had been in that place. One of them saw a shooting star and was moved to record the experience on stone.

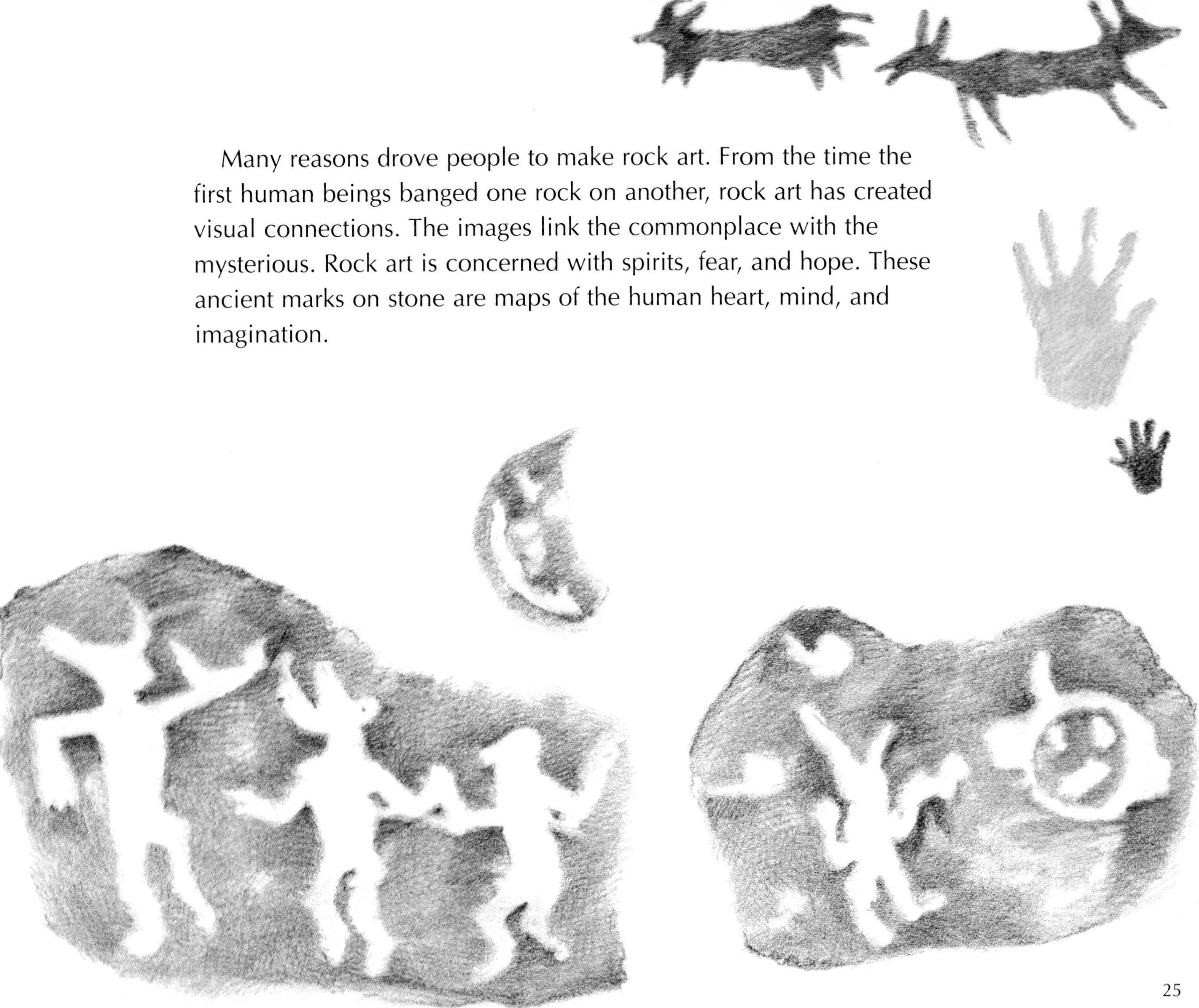

Many reasons drove people to make rock art. From the time the first human beings banged one rock on another, rock art has created visual connections. The images link the commonplace with the mysterious. Rock art is concerned with spirits, fear, and hope. These ancient marks on stone are maps of the human heart, mind, and imagination.

# The People Today

The Anasazi have not vanished, even though their many tribes and towns are buried in dust from centuries of wind blowing across the land.

They remain in a transformed way. The Pueblo people are the modern descendants of the ancient Anasazi bands who roamed, hunted, trapped, and finally settled into a farming way of life.

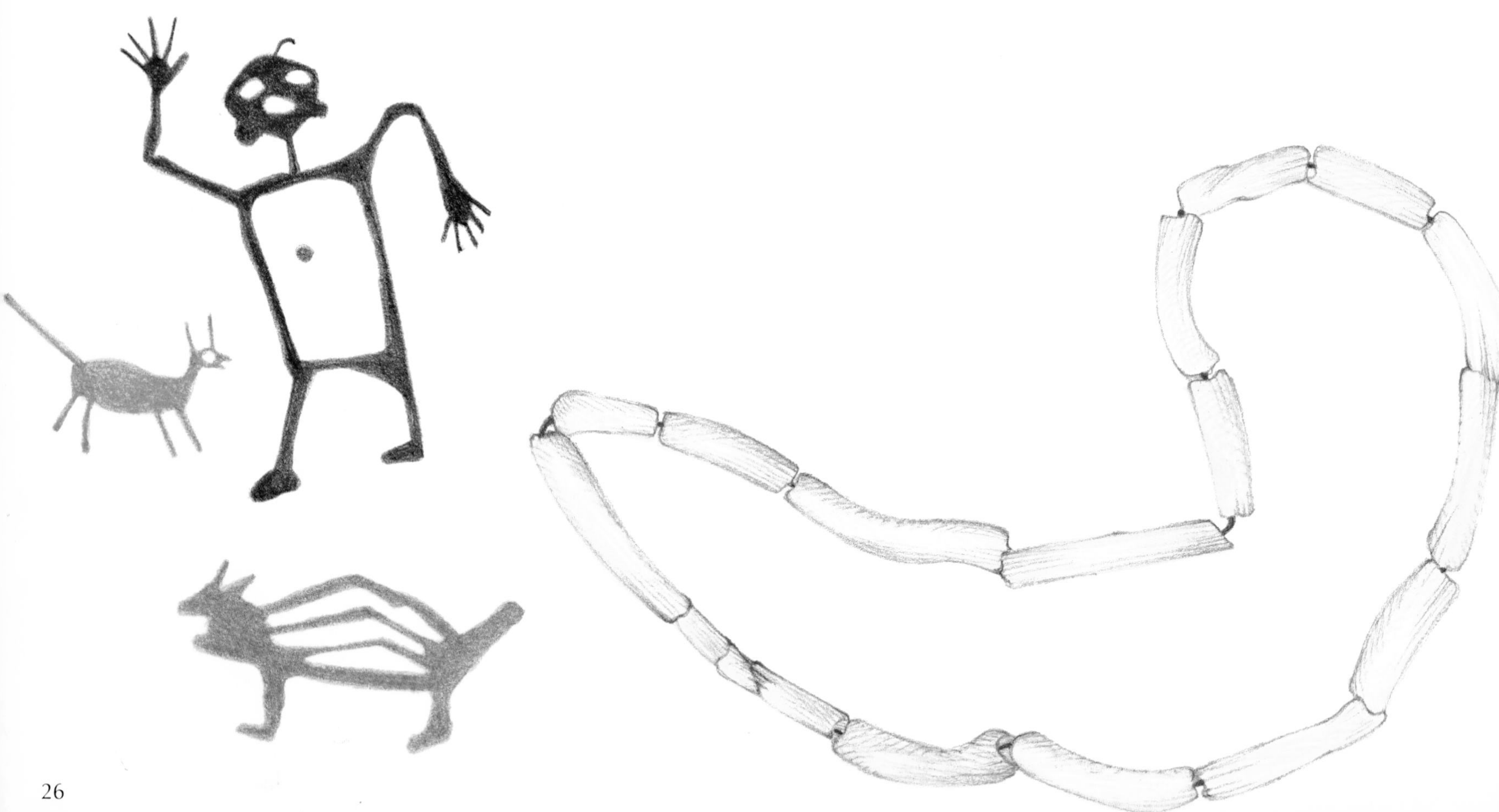

The Pueblo people live the old way, in harmony with the earth and the seasons. They continue to make art, including images on stone.

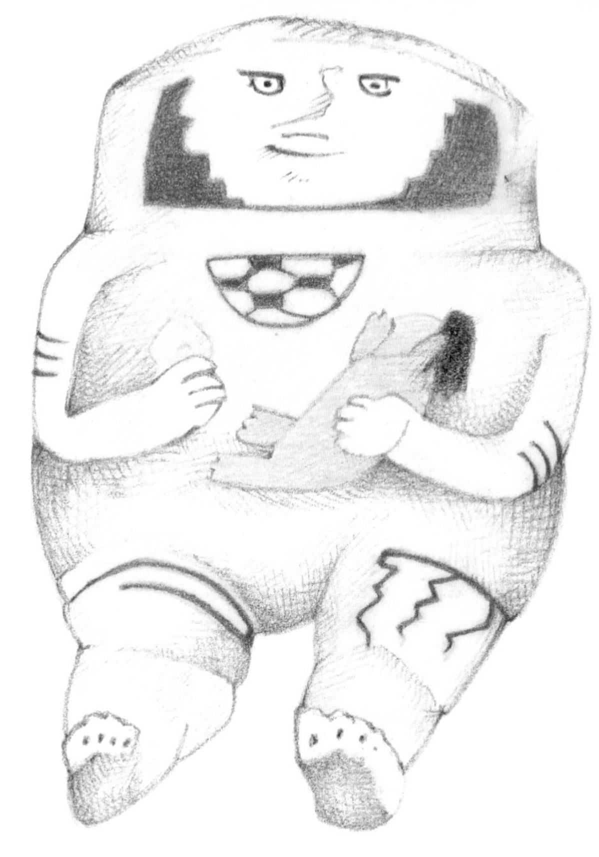

The Pueblo people are secretive and protective of their sacred works, their pictographs and petroglyphs. A friend of mine once asked a Taos Pueblo man who made the pictures on stone along the Rio Grande.

"Witches," he said, grinning.

The Pueblo people are aware of the mysterious and spiritual side of life. Even though rock art is hard to fully comprehend, because so little evidence is left to us, we still have our power to dream and imagine what these images mean now and what they once meant to those who made them.

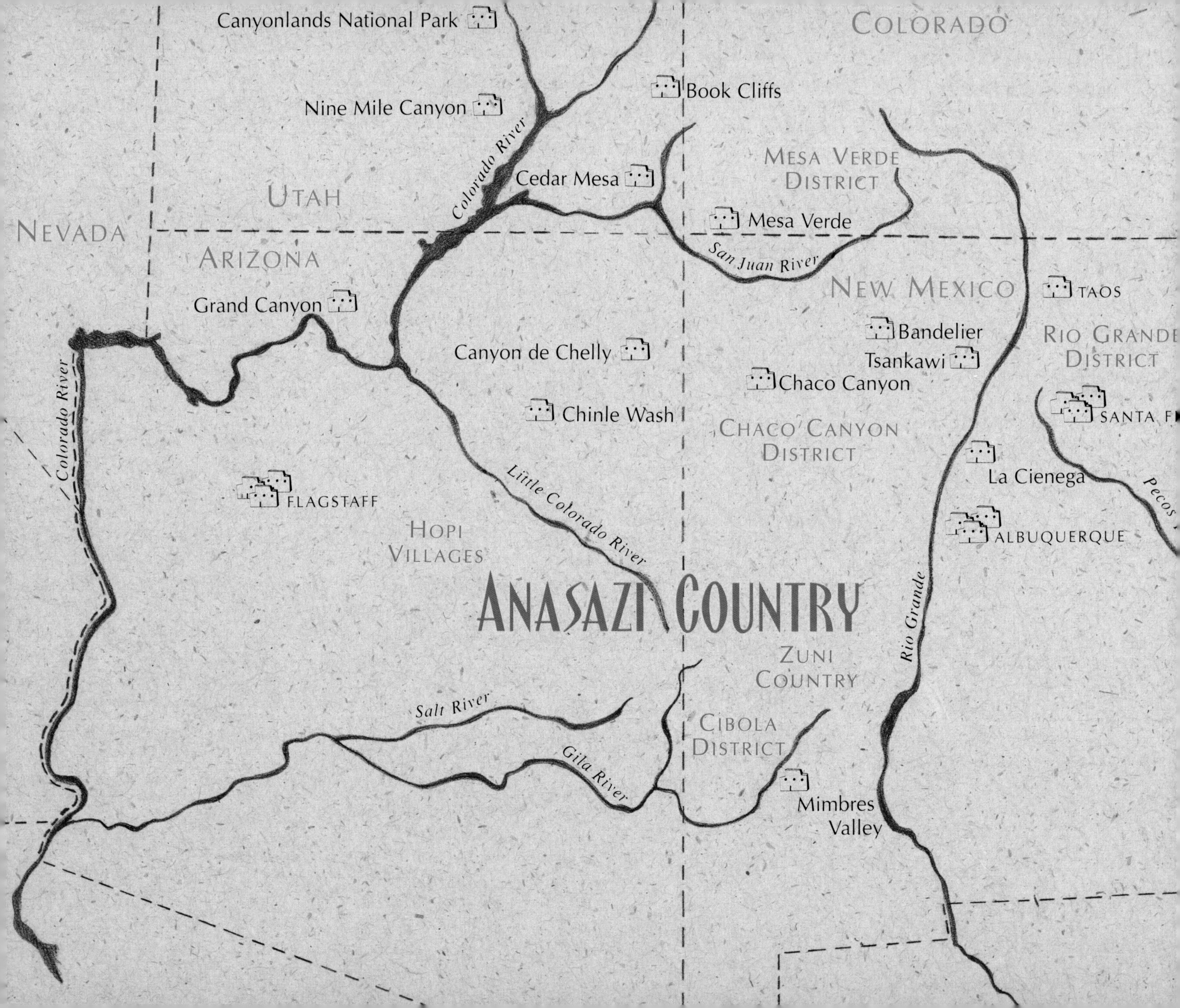

Anasazi Country
Canyonlands National Park
Colorado
Book Cliffs
Nine Mile Canyon
Colorado River
Cedar Mesa
Mesa Verde District
Utah
Mesa Verde
Nevada
Arizona
San Juan River
New Mexico
Taos
Grand Canyon
Bandelier
Rio Grande District
Canyon de Chelly
Tsankawi
Chaco Canyon
Santa F
Chinle Wash
Chaco Canyon District
Colorado River
La Cienega
Little Colorado River
Pecos
Flagstaff
Albuquerque
Hopi Villages
Rio Grande
Zuni Country
Salt River
Cibola District
Gila River
Mimbres Valley

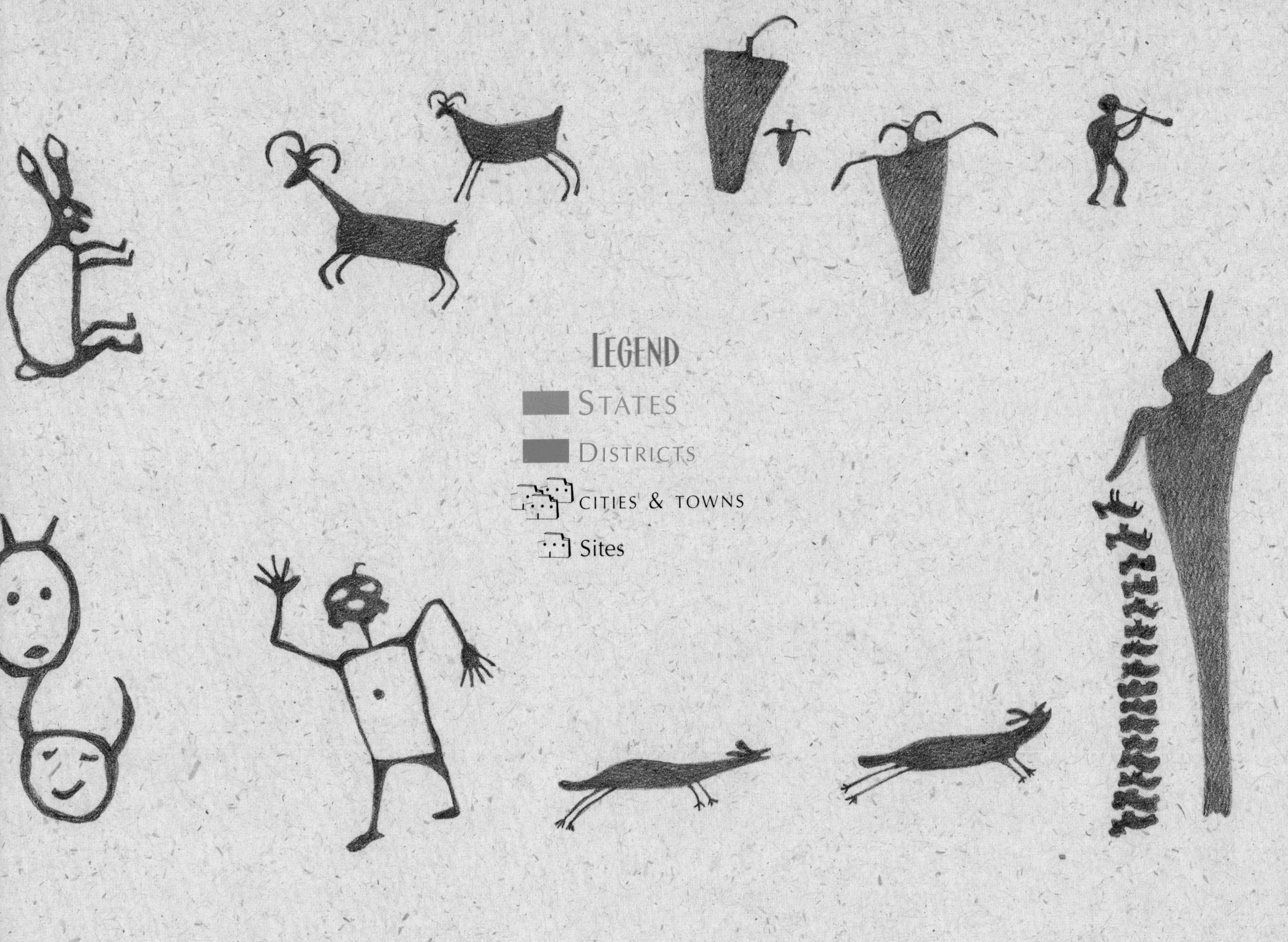
Legend
States
Districts
cities & towns
Sites

# Author's Note

Whenever you encounter a remnant of an ancient culture — a picture on a rock, the ruins of a dwelling, or a huge pyramid — remember how old it is. Be one of those people who look at the remains of the past with curiosity, respect, and no desire to do harm. Listen to the story these ancient creations tell you — and let the story be heard by the next person who comes along.